ASSOCIATED PRESS

THE HISTORY OF
TELEVISION

Text
Norm Goldstein

Photography
Associated Press

Photo Research
Axel Kessler

Design
Clive Dorman

Commissioning Editor
Andrew Preston

Publishing Assistant
Edward Doling

Editorial
Jane Adams
Louise Houghton

Production
Ruth Arthur
Sally Connolly
David Proffit
Andrew Whitelaw

Director of Production
Gerald Hughes

Director of Publishing
David Gibbon

CLB 2495
© 1991 Colour Library Books Ltd, Godalming, Surrey, England.
All rights reserved.
This 1991 edition published by Portland House,
distributed by Outlet Book Company, Inc, a Random House Company,
225 Park Avenue South, New York, New York 10003.
Color separations by Scantrans Pte Ltd, Singapore.
Printed and bound in Hong Kong.
ISBN 0 517 02011 4
8 7 6 5 4 3 2 1

ASSOCIATED PRESS

THE HISTORY OF TELEVISION

NORM GOLDSTEIN

PORTLAND HOUSE

INTRODUCTION

In a relatively brief time, television has dramatically changed the way we live. Indeed, since the beginning of civilization few inventions can claim to have had the same pervasive impact as this electronic cornucopia – the printing press and the automobile, without doubt; the telephone, maybe.

Carl Sandburg once said: "The impact of television on our culture is just indescribable. There's a certain sense in which it is nearly as important as the invention of printing."

For the past two generations, television has been arguably the most significant force for change in the collective national mind and mores. And, as Marshall McLuhan suggested, it doesn't matter what is shown on the screen; it is the medium itself that is the message.

Television today regulates – some would say, manipulates – our existence. Surveys show that most of what we know comes from watching it. National political campaigns and elections are shaped by broadcasts on television, and their candidates and issues are often introduced to us by the tube. Television molds our opinions, our eating habits, our sleeping habits, our buying habits and much of our behavior. It is society's nervous system. It connects us to the outside world, while at the same time providing an escape from it.

It has made us vicarious participants in wars and revolutions and in the aftermath of natural and accidental disasters through reports of graphic immediacy and visual intensity.

Some sixty years after taking its first steps, television now treads most of the globe with near impunity, engulfing time and thought as no other cultural phenomenon ever has. In the span of a single generation it has grown beyond the visions of its most imaginative creators from a fascinating toy to a ubiquitous tool of mass communication. Nearly every household in the United States has a television set. Americans have their sets on for an average of seven hours a day – and that time is increasing. For many the set has become a basic necessity of life. For millions of people around the world televison absorbs more time than anything else but sleep or work. There are even estimates that early in the next century it will take up more of our time than either of these.

Doomsayers predict a future of couch potatoes (or "patates des

Dr. E. F. W. Alexanderson operating the home television receiver he developed for General Electric around 1930, closely watched by his assistant, R.D.Kell.

Contestants at a dress rehearsal for "Queen for a Day" in 1950.

canapés" as they say in France), at least in the developed nations. Satirists and cartoonists warn of the future by envisioning the worst: beer-bellied sloths slaking their appetites for entertainment in an orgy of viewing at the touch of a remote control button.

This omnipresent medium began as an occasional thing, a novelty in postwar life that would be just the thing to help rebuild our private lives after the devastating global events. Even then, when it first intruded on public life, some worried about its potential. In 1938 the essayist E.B. White wrote:

"Television will enormously enlarge the eye's range, and, like radio, will advertise the Elsewhere.

"A door closing heard over the air, a face contorted, seen in a panel of light – these will emerge as the real and the true – and when we bang the door of our own cell, or look into another face

John Baird in a studio inside the Dominion Theater during a demonstration of his television system in 1937.

14

David Sarnoff standing before TV cameras in 1939, dedicating the RCA pavilion at the World's Fair.

the impression will be one of mere artifice.

"I believe television is going to be the test of the modern world and in this new opportunity to see beyond the range of our vision we shall discover either a new and unbearable disturbance of the general public or a saving radiance in the sky. We shall stand or fall by television – of that I am quite sure."

We are still standing, though perhaps a bit unsteadily, and the "testing" goes on. The influence of television continues to be debated and decried, blamed and belittled, damned and criticized, the medium itself adored and worshipped. Television has withstood dire predictions that it would abolish social life as we know it and create an illiterate society: a world of mass mediocrity peopled by observers lounging on living room sofas.

Television has changed a great deal since its birth, in both product and purpose. Programming was not the primary thought in the minds of its pioneers; the technical achievement itself was challenge enough. Later, the invention provided profits through the sale of sets. Then, of course, TV became a salesman itself – hawking everything from beer to beds, from toilet paper to trucks. Today, as TV critic and author Jeff Greenfield has pointed out, the most critical thing to understand about commercial television is what the product is.

"The product is the audience. ... The product is not the program, the product is not even the commercial. The product that television sells is us. The networks take audiences and deliver them to advertisers."

Television is no longer solely a medium of communication relaying entertainment and edification through a system that technically befuddles most of those who watch it: it has begun to control reality itself. Politicians plan according to optimal news viewing time; sponsors of sporting events bend and change rules to accommodate the networks that pay most of the fare.

Lest this desperate picture of the tube seems to portend the end of civilized living, let us not forget the paradox that is television: it can – and does – enlighten. TV showcases artistic talents, provides opportunities to widen our horizons and experiences, and often edifies. At times it can be magical. It presents the serious with the silly, the marvelous with the mundane, the exquisite with the inexcusable. It is the Great Enlightener: covering cultural and current events as does no other artificial means. It is the Great Leveler: a common denominator in modern society. It is also the Great Scapegoat: blamed for everything from poor report cards to murder and the diminishing of regional idiosyncrasies in language in favor of flat, broadcast "middle American."

It is all of these things and more ... an infinite variety show. But it is, after all, only an instrument with an "off" control as well as an "on."

Recall this from journalist Edward R. Murrow:

"The instrument can teach, it can illuminate; yes, it can even inspire. But it can do these things only to the extent that humans are determined to use it to those ends. Otherwise, it is merely lights and wires in a box."

CHAPTER I

BEGINNINGS

The beginning of the 20th century was, for the most part, a time of sunny optimism, a stolid and peaceful time ripe for individual determination and innovation.

Global peace allowed both the thinkers and the dreamers to research into the latest scientific discoveries and begin to apply them to all areas of life. This was an era when fortunes could be made through invention and hard work; nothing seemed beyond the reach of ingenuity.

Hadn't Alexander Graham Bell wrought something of a social and economic revolution with the invention of the telephone barely twenty-five years earlier? Weren't there a million miles of telephone lines in the United States alone at the beginning of the century?

Hadn't Guglielmo Marconi astonished the skeptics in 1899, when, at Signal Hill in St. John's, Newfoundland, he received the first radio signal – the letter "S" – from the other side of the Atlantic?

Hadn't Reginald Fessenden, the Canadian, begun the century by demonstrating the first radio-telephone to relay recognizable speech - no longer the dot-dash spurts of Morse – through the air?

And didn't Thomas Alva Edison continue to amaze the world, achieving much of what was previously only conceived in the mind; the electric light bulb, the phonograph, the box camera and – MOTION pictures!

Even the age-old dream of flying was within man's grasp.

Society was being dramatically changed by technology. The popular song "In My Merry Oldsmobile" reminded everyone of the revolution in transportation that had been brought about by the internal combustion engine and mass production. Olds sent four hundred cars off the assembly line in one year, sixteen hundred the next, four *thousand* the year after.

Railroad lines extended, bringing people and products closer. Steel ouput increased and farm machinery went through its own revolution. Sigmund Freud published his "Interpretation of Dreams." The literary world put forth some of its finest works, including Joseph Conrad's "Lord Jim" and Frank Baum's "The Wonderful Wizard of Oz." Theodore Dreiser introduced his "Sister Carrie" and Beatrix Potter her "The Tale of Peter Rabbit."

It was an age of optimism, an age of confidence, a time when

Dr. E. F. W. Alexanderson and his assistant R. D. Kell (on the right) inspecting the motor for the revolving disk in an experimental home television set.

18

Fred Waring with Dr. E. F. W. Alexanderson (on the right) and his first model home televison receiver.

hope for the best could be matched by an expectation of reaching it.

A reader of New York's *Daily News* in 1904 might have spotted another dream germinating. The newspaper reported that "Dr. Low talks very modestly of 'televista,' the name he has given to his 'seeing by wire' invention." (The word "television" – from ancient Greek and Latin roots for "far off" and "to see" – was apparently first used in a 1907 issue of *Scientific American* magazine.) This article in the *Daily News* astutely credited previous inventions in nurturing the vision of transmitting sight and sound simultaneously:

"Now that the photo-telegraph invented by Prof. Korn is on the eve of being introduced into general practice, we are informed of some similar inventions in the same field, all of which tend to achieve some step toward the solution of the problem of television."

The reference was to the German scientist Arthur Korn, who had tansmitted a photograph by a telegraphic circuit. He was later to send one all the way from Rome to Bar Harbor, Maine.

A 1913 hobbyist who read *Wireless World* to quench his thirst for the latest developments in that infant field could have seen this prophetic statement:

"The tele-vision, being based upon the same principles as photo-telegraphy, is possible in itself."

"Televista," "television" – even "radio vision," as some were to call it – had been believed "possible in itself" by a number of

One of the early television sets developed during experiments by General Electric in Shenectady, New York. It had a three-inch screen.

imaginative "tinkerers," many of whom had set the thinking going in the previous century. Indeed, it is impossible to trace this invention to a specific time, let alone an individual sire. It is truly the result of combined efforts.

Among those who had speculated on the subject was a twenty-four-year-old German inventor, Paul Nipkow, who had shown that television was technically feasible as early as 1884. He had devised a perforated disc through which images could be scanned by mechanical means; a rotating wheel that first broke down and then reconstructed the image.

Marconi, too, was among those interested in this fascinating, age-old concept of transmitting images. But, for the time; he concentrated on his wireless telegraphy.

Left and following page: a young lady poses as her picture is transmitted by means of photoelectric cells projecting from the apparatus directly in front of her during an early experiment with television.

Marconi's Wireless Telegraph and Signal Company, Ltd. had become the Marconi Wireless Telegraph Company, a successful commercial venture thanks to the U.S. Navy. It was a leader in its field and Marconi soon started an American branch.

By 1907 the commercial wireless was firmly established. Lee De Forest had patented the triode Audion tube, a three-element vacuum tube that provided wireless with the ability to increase transmitter and amplifier powers – crucial to the development of radio. De Forest's experimental transmission on January 13, 1910 from the Metropolitan Opera House in New York is considered the first radio broadcast to the public. However, there were of course no radio sets and the music was heard only on public receivers set up at a few city locations.

In the ensuing years, radio hobbyists, with the individualistic determination of the age, began developing the new "toy." Soon, from shack-like "studios" on rooftops and garage laboratories, radio transmissions started to reach the public at large.

Facing page: Edgar Bergen with Charlie McCarthy, one of his dummies, in 1937.

24

The technical staff of Bell
Telephone Laboratories
running final tests on aparatus
prior to television
transmission.

BELL TELEPHONE LABORATORIES

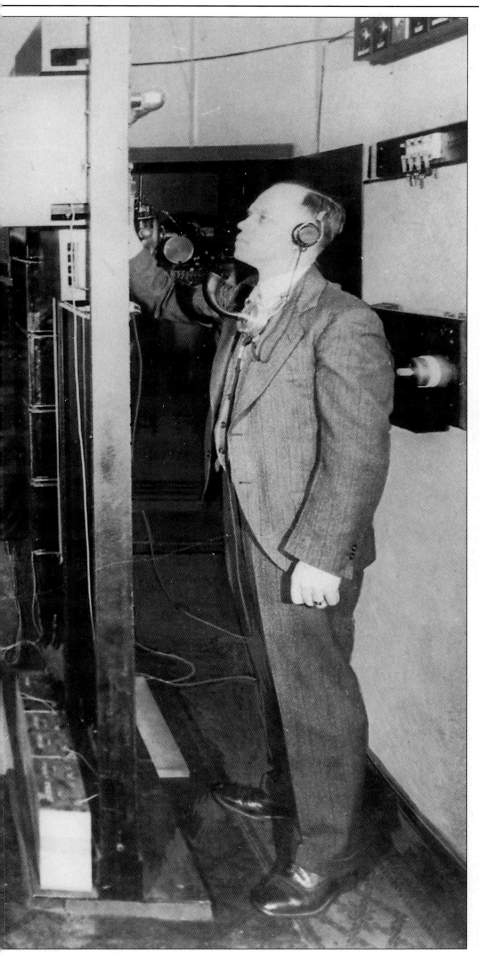

The Radio Corporation of America was established in 1919 as a joint venture of General Electric, Westinghouse, American Telephone and Telegraph and United Fruit.

It was at this time that Robert H. Goddard wrote "A Method of Reaching Extreme Altitudes," suggesting how to use rockets to reach the moon. Within a year, the RCA international communications company was handling one million words a month in overseas messages.

The 1920s, those boisterous and playful "Roaring '20s," provided the fertile times of exuberance and prosperity necessary for the nurturing of the new invention. Radio came to characterize that era of speculative imagination and confident mass production, a decade when technology, it seemed, could indeed match the visions of man.

It was in the September of 1920 that a General Electric engineer, Frank Conrad, played some phonograph music over the wireless research lab he had set up at his home in Wilkinsburg, western Pennsylvania. Something of a wireless "ham," he had been communicating with fellow hobbyists for some time, often transmitting baseball scores as well as music.

With true entrepreneurial vision, a local store used the event to advertise the sale of its wireless receivers, previously on offer in the "$10 and up" section of a Pittsburgh newspaper. Conrad's boss at G.E., vice president Harry Davis, recognized the profit potential in this and got Conrad to build a transmitter on the roof of one of the taller buildings at the company's Pittsburgh headquarters.

On October 27, 1920, the U.S. Department of Commerce assigned the call letters KDKA for that 100-watt transmitter on top of the G.E. building, making it the first official radio broadcast station. On November 2, by an arrangement to receive the news by telephone from the Pittsburgh Press, KDKA made its first broadcast. It announced the U.S. presidential election returns in Warren Harding's victory over James Cox.

WJZ in Newark, New Jersey, WBZ in Springfield,

Massachusetts, and KYW in Chicago (all Westinghouse stations) went on the air soon after.

At first the public reaction was mild; there were few receivers to pick up the output. But events like RCA's ringside transmission of the Dempsey-Carpentier boxing match in July 1921 helped awaken the public to the phenomenon to come. The "radio craze" had begun, as the industry began to see the potential for broadcasting as a force in all facets of society.

"There is radio music in the air, every night, everywhere," wrote a San Francisco newspaper. "Anybody can hear it at home on a receiving set, which any boy can put up in an hour."

Indeed, the ease and availability of "crystal sets" quickly relayed momentous events directly into a growing number of home kitchens and living rooms.

Household radio receivers, or "music boxes", like RCA's Radiola, proliferated. Radio-telegraph stations and patents, taken over by the government for the duration of World War I, were restored to their original owners in February 1920. The Bell Group, Westinghouse, International Radio Telegraph and even United Fruit joined in the competition.

26

Ventriloquist's dummies were part of John Logie Baird's equipment during his research in the 1920s.

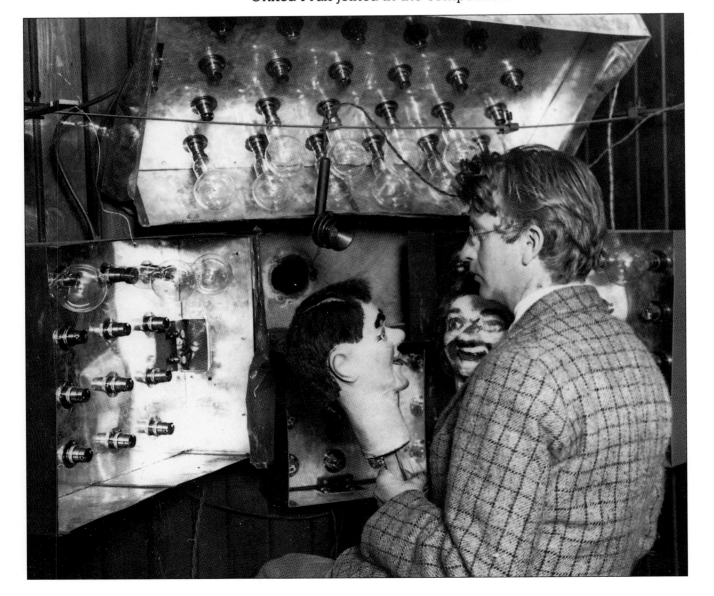

Dennis James of "People Will Talk," 1963.

By 1922, sales of radio sets, parts and accessories totaled $60 million. In 1929 those sales reached nearly $850 million, an increase of more than 1,400 percent.

Radio antennas increased in number, as did broadcast stations – which were soon to hook up nationwide. Thirty-two stations were licensed by the U.S. Department of Commerce in 1921, two hundred and fifty-four in 1922.

Programming was at first limited to music, a college football game, an opera perhaps, or some news comments from H.V. Kaltenborn. Families huddled around the set to hear Roxy and His Gang, the Happiness Boys, or Rudy Vallee.

The National Broadcasting Company was formed in 1926 and within a year had established two national networks, the "blue" and the "red." The Columbia Broadcasting System started in 1927, the same year a federal act created the Federal Radio Commission to regulate broadcasting in the United States and handle the licensing process.

The British Broadcasting Corporation had already been established in Great Britain.

While radio flourished in those years, experiments continued in the effort to marry sound and vision.

A Scottish lad by the name of John Logie Baird was one of those talented tinkerers in this new field of electronics. Born in the town of Helensburgh, not far from Glasgow, Baird attended the Royal Technical College and Glasgow University.

He later moved to London and devoted himself to experimenting with television. He had his first workable apparatus in 1924 in a tiny laboratory in Hastings where he had been studying the problems of "seeing by wireless." He had progressed to reproducing

28

E. F. Kingsbury of Bell Telephone Laboratories, talking into a microphone while being viewed by photoelectric eyes behind the three screens in front of him.

objects in outline, then the recognizable image of a human face, with light, shade and some detail. (He had experimented first with a ventriloquist's dummy because its unmarked features carried better than those of humans and it held up better under the hot lights.) In October of 1925, in John Baird's attic workroom, a historic event took place. It was the first transmission of a moving image, with grades of light and shade enabling recognition of a face. He gave his first public demonstration on January 27, 1926, to an invited audience of members of the Royal Institute of England.

The *Glasgow Herald* made due note of the local boy making good: "Mr. John L. Baird, a native of Helensburgh, recently invented an apparatus which makes television possible." Two years later this local boy was to transmit a signal from the Baird Station in Kent across the Atlantic to Hartsdale, New York.

Baird first demonstrated color television – or rather, considering the source, "colour" television – in 1928, later improving it with

Bruce DuMont, President of the Museum of Broascast Communications in Chicago, demonstrating an early 1950's Zenith entertainment center, complete with radio, turntable and television set.

an electronic apparatus. His television system was adopted by the Germans in 1929 and also by the young British Broadcasting Corporation. The British, however, later abandoned it in favor of an improved system.

The BBC made experimental broadcasts between 1929 and 1935, but they were low definition (thirty to a hundred scanning lines) and flickered badly. At Alexander Palace on November 2, 1936, the BBC opened what was considered to be the first high definition TV service (it had 405 scanning lines), and soon began regular programming.

Baird later worked on stereoptic television, but died in 1946 before it was developed.

The cast of Bob Hope's 1966 comedy special, "Murder at NBC:" (front row, left to right) Dan Rowan, Bill Dana, (behind, left to right) Milton Berle, Wally Cox, Soupy Sales, Dick Martin, Jack Carter, Hope, Jimmy Durante and Dick Shawn.

30

Many believe his early work qualifies him for the title of the "inventor" of television. He was certainly a great pioneer.

While Baird immersed himself in his experiments in Great Britain, Charles Francis Jenkins was doing similar work in the United States. He, like Baird, used a mechanical spinning disc to provide silhouette images. As early as 1923 he transmitted a picture of President Warren Harding by wireless from Washington, D.C., to Philadelphia, Pa., a distance of some one hundred miles.

It was Jenkins who had forecast in 1929: "The folks in California and Maine, and all the way in between, will be able to see the inauguration cermonies of their President in Washington, the Army and Navy [football] games on Franklin Field [in

Bess Myerson and Allen Funt, co-hosts of "Candid Camera."

32

Philo Taylor Farnsworth with one of his early operative television receivers, San Francisco, 1929.

Philadelphia] and the struggle for supremacy in our national sport, baseball."

Meanwhile, on a farm in Idaho, a youngster named Philo Taylor Farnsworth revealed an exceptional grasp of electro physics. When he was six years old he had determined that he was going to be an inventor. His playthings then were a toy dynamo and a tiny electric motor; he connected the dynamo to the flywheel of his mother's sewing machine and generated enough current to operate the motor.

By the time he was twelve he had embarked on a career of invention and moved with his family to a ranch near Rigby, Utah. There, in his chemistry class at Rigby Senior High, and later at Brigham Young University in Provo, he pored over textbooks, consulted instructors and played with every piece of electrical apparatus he could find. His dedicated pursuits resulted in a worthy brainchild: a system of transmitting images by breaking up light rays into electrons and reassembling them at some distant point.

Philo T. Farnsworth in his laboratory in 1938 with a modern camera tube.

Philo T. Farnsworth at work in 1940 as director of research for Farnsworth Television and Radio Corporation, Fort Wayne, Indiana.

In 1924, at the age of eighteen, he had worked out the concepts of a television system. It was then that he met George Everson, who was organizing the community chest campaign in Salt Lake City, Utah. Farnsworth joined his staff and later told him of his ambition to perfect a practical system of television. The key, he told Everson, was not developing a system by mechanical means like the revolving discs – "they're barking up the wrong tree" – but rather by harnessing and controlling electrons. Just as the harrow goes back and forth in the fields, the farm boy believed, leaving lines in the freshly turned soil, electrons could be bounced back and forth in a vacuum tube. This would enable him to break an image down line by line and convert it into an electronic signal.

34

Everson understood little of electronics, but was nevertheless impressed with the young man. He eventually provided the financial wherewithal to continue the research work and build the expensive apparatus needed to demonstrate it. Farnsworth and his bride, Elma Gardner, moved to California and turned one room of their apartment into a laboratory and installed generators in the garage. Secrecy surrounded the work, with dining room shades drawn during the daytime. Once, a neighbor suspicious of the "mysterious-looking" packages constantly arriving and being carried into the house, called the police. It was 1926, Prohibition was in full swing and the Farnsworth's became suspected of a possible illegal whiskey operation. As the story goes, two policemen investigated and searched the house before being convinced that, though a bit eccentric, the goings-on were not illegal.

When Philo was ready, Everson brought the law firm of Lyon & Lyon into the picture. They met with Farnsworth and Dr. Mott Smith, a scientist on the faculty of the California Institute of Technology.

At the end of the explanation given by Farnsworth, Everson asked the technical men:

"Is this thing scientifically sound?"

"Yes," was the reply.

"Is this idea original?'"

"Startingly so. We know of no other research along these lines."

Smith added: "I don't know how this will work out commercially – certainly you may expect to encounter great difficulties – but the boy's work is not only scientifically sound, it is startingly original and staggering in its implications."

Farnsworth's first application for a television patent, covering a complete television system – including his most significant "dissector," or cathode ray tube – was made on January 7, 1927. The dissector was capable of dividing an image into parts, the light values of which could be restored to form a reproduction of the original picture.

The first effective transmission of Farnsworth's image motion system was in 1929 and showed cigarette smoke. He moved to Philadelphia to work in a Philco laboratory and continue his television tests on motion picture films. Footage of Mary Pickford combing her hair and the "long count" in the disputed Demspey-

A reproducton of an image transmitted by electrical scanning in the Farnsworth laboratories in Philadelphia in 1935. The original image appeared on the flat end of a cathode ray tube and measured six by eight inches.

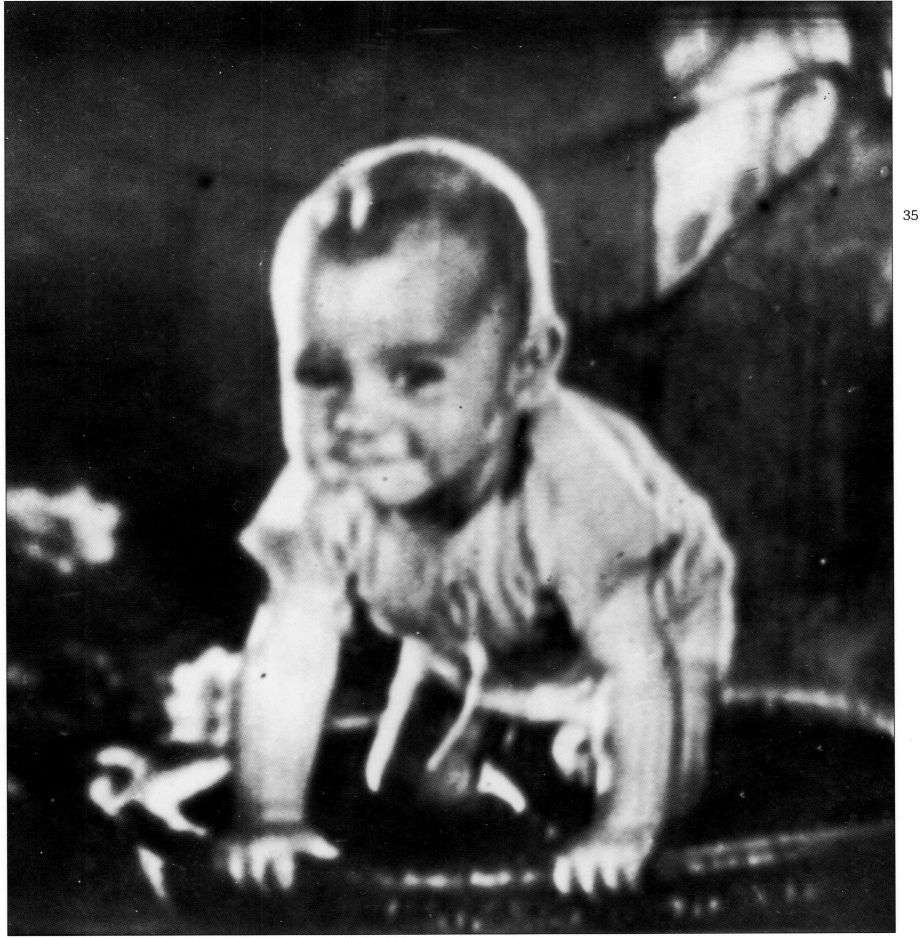

Tunney heavyweight boxing match was his source.

In 1930 – when he was still just twenty-one – Philo Farnsworth patented the cathode ray scanner, the electronic method which became the basis of modern television tubes. (He sued before RCA gave him credit – and royalties – for inventing the basic principles of the television camera tube.) The first public demonstration of his electronic television system was made in the summer of 1934 at the Franklin Institute in Philadelphia.

Farnsworth is credited with more than two hundred U.S. and foreign patents, including those for scanning, synchronizing, focusing, contrasting, controls and power.

Pioneers: an Idaho farm boy, a Scottish engineer ... and two Russian émigrés.

Vladimir Kosma Zworykin was born in Russia in 1889 in the small town of Mouron, on the Oka River, where his father owned and operated a fleet of boats. He was an electrical engineering graduate of the Petrograd Institute of Technology. He had studied

36

This portable TV set of 1954 plugged into a car's cigarette lighter socket.

William Boyd as "Hopalong Cassidy."

Facing page: Flipper the dolphin, TV star of the '60s, with his trainer and a young contest winner at the Miami Seaquarium.

with Professor Boris Rosing, one of the first to develop the concept of television by electronic, rather than mechanical, means. Zworykin was later to become a radio expert in the Russian Army Signal Corps during World War I.

Zworykin emigrated to the United States in 1919, became a naturalized citizen, and joined the Westinghouse Electric Corporation. There, at laboratories in Princeton, New Jersey, he invented the first practical television transmission tube, the iconoscope. It used photoelectric effects – the ejection of electrons by the action of light – as the basis for scanning and converting images into electric currents.

In 1924, a year after filing for a patent for the iconoscope, he filed another for the kinescope, his television receiver. The iconoscope greatly reduced the amount of light needed to capture an image and became the heart of the first practical television camera. (It was later superseded by the image orthicon tube.)

The first demonstration of his iconoscope took place in 1924 at the Westinghouse Electric and Manufacturing Company in Pittsburgh, where he was a research engineer.

Zworykin described that showing to the executives of Westinghouse thus:

"I was terribly excited and proud, but after a few days I was informed, very politely, that my demonstration had been extremely interesting, but that it might be better if I were to spend my time on something a little more useful."

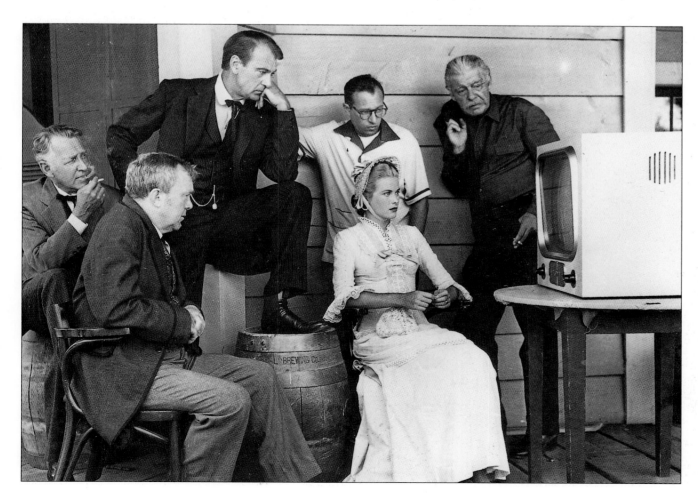

In 1951, television coverage of the baseball World Series tore the cast of "High Noon" away from their work: (left to right) Otto Kruger, Thomas Mitchell, Gary Cooper, an unidentified studio worker, Grace Kelly and Lon Chaney Jr.

When he demonstrated a more refined system, including the kinescope, five years later, Westinghouse was still not impressed. So Zworykin joined RCA that year – the year he got his first patent for color television. It was there that he met the man later to be called the "prophet and principal backer" of television, David Sarnoff.

Sarnoff was born in the village of Uzlian in the Russian province of Minsk. When he was nine years old, his family made its way to New York, like so many others fleeing from the czar. Making a penny any way he could while growing up in New York's teeming Lower East Side, Sarnoff eventually became an office boy with American Marconi. He learned the wireless telegraph and was there when the *Titanic* sank in the Atlantic after hitting an iceberg in 1912. He spent most of three days relaying the news received by wireless from the S.S. *Olympic*.

He moved up in the organization and by 1919, when RCA was created out of American Marconi and G.E., he was an important cog. He was instrumental in the development of radio in those years, shaping RCA into the giant of the fledgling industry, well above all competitors.

He also dreamed of the day sight could be added to the sound.

Sarnoff had seen the possibilities as early as 1923. In a memorandum to RCA directors he wrote:

"I believe that television, which is the technical name for seeing instead of hearing by radio, will come to pass in due course."

40

Lawrence Welk, his orchestra and singers.

David Sarnoff and Guglielmo Marconi (on the right) on a visit to the RCA Communications transmitting center at Rocky Point, Long Island, in 1933.

42

The "Dance Show" episode of "Laverne and Shirley" in 1978, with (left to right) Penny Marshall as Laverne, David Lander as Squiggy, Cindy Williams as Shirley and Michael McKean as Lenny.

(How much *has* come to pass is underscored by his definition of the word "television" as "the technical name.")

He went on: "It is not too much to expect that in the near future when news is telegraphed by radio ... a picture of the event will likewise be sent over by radio and both will arrive simultaneously, thus ... we will be able to see as well as read in New York, within an hour or so, the event taking place in London, Buenos Aires or Tokyo.

"I also believe that transmission and reception of motion pictures by radio will be worked out within the next decade. ...

"The problem is technically similar to that of radio telephony, though of more complicated nature; but within the range of technical achievement. Therefore, it may be that every broadcast

receiver will also be equipped with a television adjunct by which the instrument will make it possible for those at home to see as well as hear what is going on at the broadcast station."

Sarnoff became chief salesman of the potential of television.

He told a University of Missouri audience in 1924 that there would come a day when a family could sit in the comfort of their own home and see and hear a play being staged hundreds of miles away. Similarly, they might hear a sermon and see "every play of emotion on the preacher's face as he exhorts the congregation to the path of religion."

He went even further in 1927: "If we let our imagination plunge ahead, we may also dream of television in faithful colors."

A memorable year, 1927: Charles Lindbergh, the "Lone

Hal Linden (center) in a 1981 episode of the ABC series "Barney Miller," in which he took the title role and Ron Carey (right) was Officer Levitt. Michael Tucci is playing the culprit.

Eagle," enraptured the world with the first solo, nonstop flight across the Atlantic in his monoplane *Spirit of St. Louis*. Aviation was the theme of "Wings," a movie starring Clara Bow and Buddy Rogers which was to win the first Best Picture Oscar. Popular songs like "The Best Things in Life Are Free," "Blue Skies" and "I'm Looking Over a Four-Leaf Clover," reflected the elan of the era. Babe Ruth hit sixty home runs for the New York Yankees, and the first talkie, "The Jazz Singer," premiered in New York.

That same year, indistinct pictures, sent by wire, were developed enough for an interstate transmission. U.S. Secretary of Commerce Herbert Hoover, in Baltimore, Maryland, was seen on a tiny screen in the New York office of Walter Gifford, president of American Telephone & Telegraph. His voice, however, was transmitted by telephone.

44

Vladimir Zworykin with a cathode ray tube in 1937.

Ernest F.W. Alexanderson led G.E. program experiments in Schenectady, New York. He inaugurated the first regular television broadcast on May 11, 1928, through WGY. A few months later, the station aired a melodrama called "The Queen's Messenger," viewed on an experimental screen four inches wide and three inches high.

David Sarnoff was a vice president of RCA when Vladimir Zworykin came to demonstrate his achievements in 1929.

Sarnoff watched and finally said:

"It's too good to be true. What will it cost to develop the idea?"

"Maybe $100,000," Zworykin answered.

"All right, it's worth it," Sarnoff declared.

Sarnoff was often to say that RCA spent $50 million before it ever got a penny back from TV.

E. F. W. Alexanderson (on the right) with members of the cast of the first drama ever broadcast on television. It was shown by WGY on September 11, 1928.

46

Zworykin later became the director of electronic research at RCA. His system is the basis of television as we know it.

The year before he died (at the age of ninety-two), he was asked about the content of his "child," American television.

"Awful," was his ironic reply.

But he was prominent among those men, those talented tinkerers, those dreamers of the dream, who made television possible some sixty years ago.

And it was the support, patronage and encouragement of "General" David Sarnoff that made it happen.

Zworykin first exhibited his system – using an iconoscope with a cathode ray tube – at the convention of the Institute of Radio Engineers at Rochester, New York, in November 1929. It received little attention and less enthusiasm.

There was much experimentation yet to be done to improve quality, performance and definition; television remained a "sometime" thing – not yet ready for prime time. The dreams were dimmed, it was the global economic depression of the 1930s. But they never dimmed that much.

The dream of television was never far from the plans of RCA, Farnsworth's company, the Allen B. DuMont laboratories, Bell, CBS, General Electric, Philco, Zenith and others.

An experimental transmission by NBC in 1930 used the cartoon figure of Felix the Cat as its subject. In a scheduled TV program on July 21, 1931, New York Mayor Jimmy Walker

Felix the Cat, star of NBC's first experimental telecast in 1930.

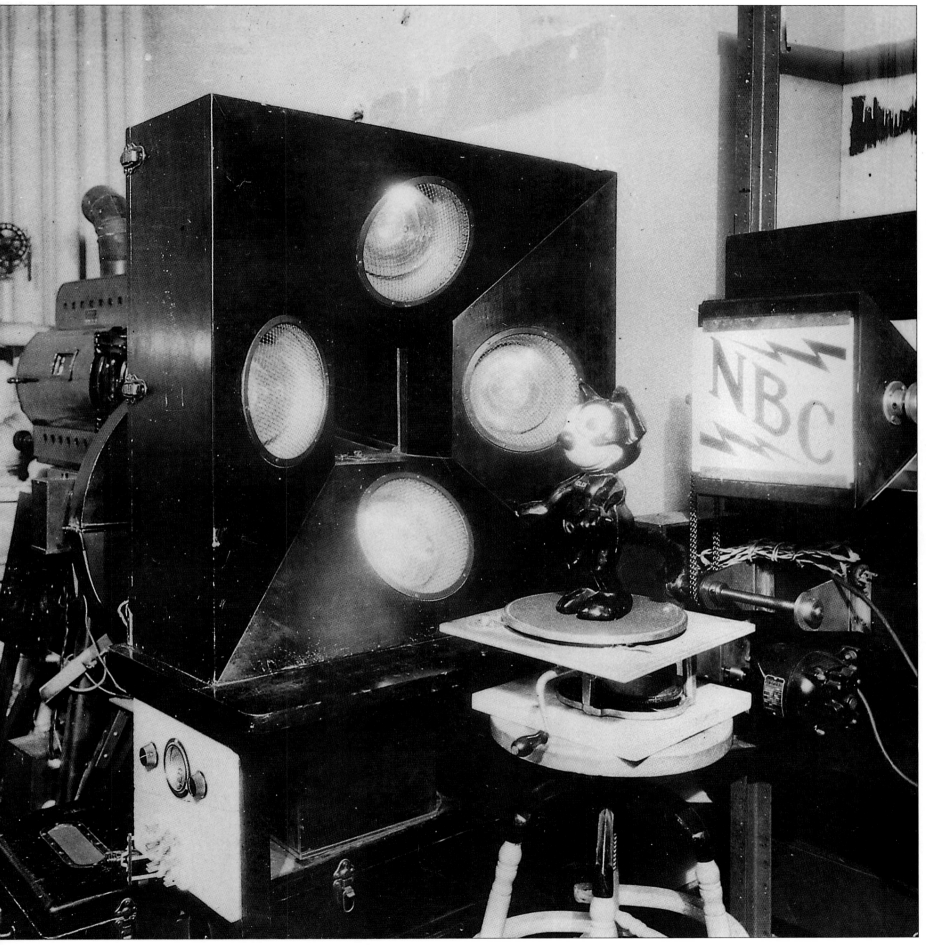

Lawyer Perry Mason (on the left, played by Raymond Burr) having a game of chess with District Attorney William Talman on the "Perry Mason Show."

Facing page: Peewee, a toy Boston Bulldog, watching his mistress, Doris Brownlee, in a test on a home receiving cabinet in the San Francisco laboratory of the Farnsworth Television Company.

introduced a variety of acts, from George Gershwin on the piano to Kate Smith singing "When the Moon Comes Over the Mountain." And in 1932, presidential election returns were televised, with the victory of Franklin D. Roosevelt over Herbert Hoover.

Crucial to the development of television at this time was the work of Edwin H. Armstrong. It was Armstrong's introduction of FM (frequency modulation radio waves), along with his methods of improving the range of sounds able to be transmitted, that brought television yet another step closer to public acceptance. He also worked successfully on eliminating static.

In the latter part of the decade, Dr. C.C. Clark, an associate professor of general science at the N.Y.U. School of Commerce, lectured on photo-electricity as students watched him on TV screens. They were able to ask him questions through a special talk-back radio circuit.

NBC showed excerpts from the Broadway show "Susan and God" (with Gertrude Lawrence) and also shot scenes of the construction of the new Rockefeller Center. While working on the latter, cameramen captured the tragic sight of a woman falling from the eleventh floor of the building.

CBS began installing a TV transmitter atop the Chrysler Building in New York to relay signals from their studio in Grand Central Terminal. The General Electric station was already set up near Schenectady, New York, and DuMont Laboratories was building a TV station in Passaic, New Jersey, sharing time with an NBC transmitter atop the Empire State Building.

50

Left: the parties, celebrity guest stars, exotic locations and romantic storylines of "Show Boat" ensured its success. Left to right: Fred Grandy (Gopher), Patricia Klous (Judy), Ted McGinley (Ace), Gavin Macleod (Captain Stubing), Bernie Kopell (Doc), Jill Whelan (Vicki) and Ted Lange (Isaac).

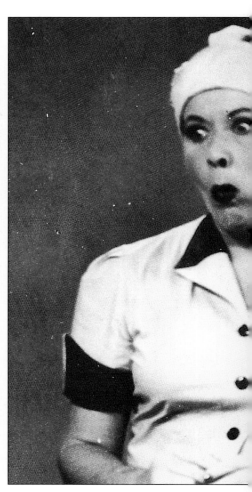

The future of television, though glimpsed only in fits and starts, was getting clearer, clear enough for the federal government to pass the Communications Act, which included TV, in 1934. The Federal Communications Commission was introduced to succeed the Radio Commission.

The British were far from idle in their continuing experiments in the '30s. Baird demonstrated his "multi-television system" by showing a variety performance at the Dominion Theatre early in 1937. The screen was described as a "visual loudspeaker," and provided an enlarged image of the entertainer that was able to be seen by the "biggest audience." The BBC was by then offering regular television programming to about fourteen thousand subscribers.

In May 1937, the coronation pageant of King George VI had been broadcast to those who could get close enough to the public receivers set up near the parade area.

A reporter visiting the Radiolympia exhibition, "the mammoth eye and ear show," at Olympic Coliseum in London in 1938, spoke of a hundred television sets, "all operating efficiently." The prices ranged from $150 to $1,000 for the sets, he noted, and the screens varied "from the tiny, pocket camera print size to twenty-four by nineteen inches on a console combined with all wave receiver, which may be observed satisfactorily by 100 persons in a room 30 feet square." It was also noted, however, that three problems had to be solved before television became a

Lucille Ball (on the right) with Vivian Vance (on the left) in the chocolate factory episode of the "I Love Lucy Show."

52

Members of the Federal Communications Commission inspecting a "portable" TV set at a demonstration in Washington, D.C.

necessity in Britain: transmission to regional stations; cost of sets; improvement in the variety of programs.

Eleven image transmitters had been licensed experimentally in the United States by the end of 1938.

Indeed, 1938 was the year in which American field tests were accepted as proof that television was ready for the home. That became the promise of 1939. The World's Fair in New York in 1939 was introduced thus:

"Outdoor television is clearly 1938's most important technical contribution to the progress of the infant art ... Undoubtedly, the

next year will bring with it numerous improvements that make for clearer and brighter images, but the principles of the all electronic system have passed through their practical test period and been found satisfactory. I do not hestitate, therefore, in saying that television is ready technically for its public introduction."

The drums of war in Europe seemed muted in the United States in 1939. Indeed, as the British and French challenged the Germans, Americans, though deeply concerned, escaped to the movies. They saw such eventual classics as "Gone With The Wind," "Wuthering Heights," "Mr. Smith Goes To Washington,"

CBS's early radio stars included (top, left to right) Orson Welles (1938), Janette Davis and Arthur Godfrey (1949), Kate Smith and Babe Ruth (1936), (bottom, left to right) Walter Winchell (1930), Bing Crosby, and Matthew Crowley as Buck Rogers (1936).

"Goodbye Mr. Chips," "Gunga Din," "Ninotchka" and "The Hunchback of Notre Dame." They were also singing the bouncy "Beer Barrel Polka" and the patriotic "God Bless America" and "Over the Rainbow" from the film "The Wizard of Oz."

The theme of the 1939 World's Fair was similarly magical and optimistic: "The World of Tomorrow." Its symbols were a trylon – a spike reaching more than six hundred feet high – and a perisphere – actually a globular theater. Visitors to the site in Queens, New York, were delighted by the parachute jump and Billy Rose's Aquacade, and entertained by "Les Brown and His Band of Renown" and its vocalists, Jack Haskell and Doris Day. They would have also seen a model of an artificial heart, a

One of two vans used by NBC in 1937 to make the first experimental pickups of outdoor news events.

54

Facing page: a television in a clear glass cabinet and with an eight-by-ten-inch screen attracted a lot of attention at the 1939 World's Fair.

compact car from Crosley, automatic milking machines, aerated bread and demonstrations of man-made lightning.

On April 30, 1939, in the Court of Peace at the opening of the World's Fair, the President of the United States faced a television camera for the first time. It was the birth of a new industry. About a thousand viewers, scattered throughout a fifty-mile radius of New York, watched that bright, sunny day on an estimated one hundred or two hundred receivers. The telecast opened just after

56

noon with a long shot of the trylon and perisphere, then provided a panorama of gathering crowds, fountains and waving flags. Two NBC mobile television vans were at the scene, one a transmitter relaying signals to the Empire State Building, the other handling the pick-up. They were attached by coaxial cable with the camera on the platform, about fifty feet from the speaker, President Franklin D. Roosevelt. Secret Service would not allow the cameras to get closer.

President Franklin D. Roosevelt, at the opening of the World's Fair, addressing the crowd at the Court of Peace.

"Every detail was distinct, even the fleecy texture of the clouds," lauded one newspaper critic.

Then, speaking at the dedication of the RCA Building at the Fair, David Sarnoff said: "It is with a feeling of humbleness that I come to the moment of announcing the birth in this country of a new art so important in its implications that it is bound to affect all society.

"It is an art which shines like a torch in a troubled world.

"It is a creative force which we must learn to utilize for the benefit of all mankind.

"This miracle of engineering skills which one day will bring the world to the home also brings a new American industry to serve

David Sarnoff standing before TV cameras to dedicate the RCA pavilion at the 1939 World's Fair.

58

man's material welfare. Television will become an important factor in American economic life."

These pronouncements more than fifty years ago must have seemed more bravura than realism then with the world standing precariously on the edge of global war. Yet they were to prove to be understated prophecy – and in a dramatically short time too. The radio industry placed that day, April 30, 1939, on a par with November 2, 1920, when they marked the Election Day broadcast from KDKA as the beginning of the "radio craze."

Television sets went on sale that April 30, with prices ranging from $200 for a four-by-five-inch screen to $1,000 for the largest console, equipped with thirty-six tubes and a seven-by-ten-inch screen. An attachment to convert a broadcast receiver into a television instrument cost $200.

When viewers were returned from that visionary "World of Tomorrow" at the World's Fair, they could tune in on a boxing

The television image of David Sarnoff at the dedication ceremony of the RCA pavilion at the 1939 World's Fair.

match between Jack Pembridge and Pat Dunne, televised from a roped arena in the R.C.A. studio. Former heavyweight boxing champion Max Baer and Bill Stern were the announcers. (Pembridge won the three–rounder by decision.)

60   Viewers learned that studio presentations from Radio City would be telecast on Wednesdays and Fridays from 8-9 p.m., and that there would be an outdoor pickup at the Fair on Wednesday, Thursday and Friday afternoons. One of those telecasts showed King George VI and Queen Elizabeth at the Fair.

On May 17, 1939, NBC put a television camera on a twelve-foot-high wooden stand at Baker Field in Manhattan. With announcer Bill Stern at the microphone and a sixteen-man crew they presented the first televised sporting event in history. Viewers within a fifty-mile radius were able to watch the Princeton baseball team beat Columbia 2-1 in ten innings. On August 26, NBC telecast the first baseball game, between the Brooklyn Dodgers and the Cincinnati Reds at Brooklyn's Ebbets Field.

The few hundred people who had bought television receivers got a limited program schedule throughout the rest of that year and 1940. At this time a new car might cost about $1,000; a new TV set about $650, with virtually nothing to watch on it. Radio audiences, meanwhile, were delighted with the antics of Jack Benny and Eddie Cantor, "The Shadow," "Fibber McGee and Molly," "Amos 'n Andy" and the "Burns and Allen Show."

CBS demonstrated color television to the press and the FCC on August 27, 1940, with its first public demonstration in January the following year.

Despite the war in Europe, television was gradually growing. There were numerous court fights, primarily over conflicts in technical standards. Then, on April 30, 1941, the FCC authorized unrestricted commercial television and assigned eighteen channels for that purpose. By the end of the year, one million TV sets had been sold and the Bulova watch manufacturers had provided the first TV commercial.

The first commercial television station, WNBT, New York, began broadcasts to about forty-seven hundred TV-set-owners. Programming included regular TV news with Lowell Thomas.

Then reality intruded: war. All production came to a halt and the national focus was on one target.

Scenes of the wedding between heiress Nina Cortlandt (played by Taylor Miller) and Dr. Cliff Warner (Peter Bergman) in "All My Children," 1980.

CHAPTER II

BIGGER AND BETTER

"So you come to the end of the war and here's what you have: You have a country that is desperate, hungry for privacy, for an end to enforced congregations. You have a whole series of forces leading to the development of more isolated, private pleasures in living.

"Television, then, becomes absolutely a perfect part of this, a perfect, perfect device for the time."

So wrote television critic and author Jeff Greenfield in his analysis of the reasons for the startling growth of television after World War II.

Indeed, everything seemed to dovetail at once and television as a dominant influence on society scurried apace. There were now four networks competing in the broadcasting industry. NBC was ordered by the FCC to give up its "blue" network, which was sold to Edward J. Noble in 1943 and became the American Broadcasting Company (ABC). The DuMont network had been created in 1946 by Allen B. DuMont, who had previously worked with Charles Jenkins on his early TV experiments. DuMont owned three stations, in New York, Washington and Pittsburgh. (The network went out of business in 1955.)

The end of the war freed materials again and manufacturers were ready and eager to meet the new consumer demands. The FCC resumed licensing of television stations, approving twenty-four new ones by mid-1946. Advertising agencies revved up, too, many creating special television departments for commercials and programming.

What an event it became to bring home a TV receiver in those heady post-war days! A TV owner immediately took a step up in class, envied by all those who noticed "the box" being delivered (or carried) home. The have-nots were willing to befriend even the ordinary ornery who might be fortunate enough to have one.

Urban areas became forests of rooftop antennas, plucking signals from the sky (though most often indistinctly) and relaying them through wires that climbed down the sides of buildings like ivy. These wires found their way to the back of a box that housed a further technological tangle of tubes. Indoor antenna – more often called "rabbit ears" for their pointy, two-pronged shape – required a contortionist, not an engineer. The instrument had to be held at just the right angle if viewers were to be able to

The TV generation: children growing up with the new medium in 1949.

64

With the war over, the buying spree for home television sets began in earnest, and they became the big gift of Christmas '48.

differentiate between a baseball team and a symphony orchestra. Owners became instant experts in repair and maintenance; do-it-yourselfers became as familiar with horizontal and vertical holds, contrast and brightness tuners as VCR aficionados are with fast forward and replay buttons today.

In December 1945, fortunate set owners could see the first three-station network telecast of the Army v Navy football game from Philadelphia. It was watched by the "largest audience on record," adding several thousand more spectators to the one hundred thousand in attendance at Municipal Stadium.

A reporter noted: "It wasn't at all difficult to follow the play, see the arrival of the President Truman and the pre-game ceremonies. However, due to the relay link, detail was not as sharp as with a direct pickup of a local contest. The best images were those supplied by the newly-developed image orthicon, sometimes called a 'noction,' because of its ability 'to see' in the dusk of a fall day. Altogether, three cameras were used, two of the ordinary type doing most of the pickup."

(The image orthicon tube was often called the "Immy," providing the inspiration for the American television awards known as "Emmys.")

The football game telecast was arranged by NBC and the Curtis Publishing Company. WNBT in New York was fed by Bell Telephone's coaxial cable, which linked the city with Philadelphia. The announcers were Red Barber and Bob Stanton.

While telecasting was still taking its first shaky steps, engineers were looking ahead to color.

It was in 1945 that Dr. Peter C. Goldmark, director of engineering research and development for CBS, announced that color TV was ready for the public through a new transmitter in the Chrysler Building. This new transmitter could also provide black-and-white pictures, "with more than twice as much picture detail as imparted with the pre-war system."

Department stores promised that the five-by-seven-inch screen of this TV set could "be viewed in a normally-lighted room." On sale in 1945 at a price of $100, it was considered to be the first moderately-priced set to be mass produced.

65

But RCA estimated it would be two years before it could manufacture sets for the public which would receive color.

Lee De Forest, the "father of radio," was among those granted a patent on a new color television system. But color television was still in the future. It didn't come into general use until about 1954 in the United States, 1960 in Japan, and 1967 in Great Britain.

In 1946 there were seven thousand black-and-white sets in the United States, all be they mostly "peephole" size with "snowy" images. But there wasn't much to be seen on them anyway, aside from an occasional special sports event like the Joe Louis-Billy Conn fight on June 19. In "prime-time" hours that year (7 p.m. to 11 p.m.) the four networks (ABC, CBS, RCA and DuMont) totalled scarcely ten hours of programming.

Most popular programmes were boxing and wrestling; there could be as many as six boxing shows on in one week. The sports suited the fledgling medium well, the area to be covered by the cameras was small and restricted. Not surprisingly, barrooms were the heaviest buyers of TV sets.

NBC's "Cavalcade of Sports," announced by Bob Stanton (later it became the "Gillette Cavalcade of Sports"), was the first of the regular boxing shows, appearing twice a week. The shows, on Monday and Friday nights, originated in New York, at St. Nicholas Arena and Madison Square Garden. "Cavalcade" lasted fourteen years.

66

Russ Hodges, announcer of the Tournament of Champions boxing on CBS in 1949.

NBC's television studio in the Rockefeller Center, New York, in 1948.

A studio in CBS's "Television City," Hollywood.

68

Wrestling star "Gorgeous George" Wagner, an early TV favorite. He traveled with a beautician and a valet and was well known for his fancy robes.

CBS ran a Wednesday night boxing show with Russ Hodges, and then Ted Husing. Dennis James, who worked for the DuMont network, was probably the best known of the early boxing and wrestling announcers. He later went on to become a popular game show host on, among others, "What's My Line," "Chance of a Lifetime," and "The Name's the Same."

(In later years commentators included Chris Schenkel, Jack Drees, Don Dunphy and, yes, Howard Cosell.)

Most popular were the wrestlers, however. "Gorgeous" George Wagner and Antonio "Argentina" Rocca became as familiar to viewers as J.R. Ewing of "Dallas" was to be in later years.

"Gorgeous" George appeared in robes of chartreuse or salmon-colored silks, with gold-plated and sequined bobby pins; a hulk presenting a more fashionable image than the lady wrestlers who followed him on the tube. By 1947 there were one hundred and seventy-eight thousand more TV sets. Also by this time, RCA had demonstrated black and white reproduction on a fifteen-by-

Rehearsing for the TV play "Guilty Bystander" in 1949 were (left to right) artistes Zachary Scott, Mary Boland and Faye Emerson, with executive producer Edmund Dormann and director Joseph Warner.

69

twenty-foot theater screen and showed seven-and-a-half-by-ten-foot color television pictures in a demonstration in Philadelphia.

There were six regularly operating television stations in the country, all in the East; New York City; Schenectady, New York; Philadelphia and Chicago. The FCC issued operating licenses to fifty-five more stations and was processing other applications, but programming had not yet hit its stride. The New York Yankees-Brooklyn Dodgers World Series (the Yankees won in seven games) and the opening of Congress televised for the first time meant there was a bit more on during prime evening hours. There was still enough time for family members to talk to each other and for the kids to get their homework done without distractions, however.

1947 was the year of the "Kraft Television Theater," a drama anthology that premiered on NBC on May 7 with a play called "Double Doors," starring John Baragrey. It became one of the most prestigious of all television programmes, presenting six hundred and fifty plays in more than eleven years on the air. All of its presentations were live. Over the years it offered plays by Shakespeare, Ibsen, Tennessee Williams and Rod Serling, and starred the likes of E.G. Marshall, Jack Lemmon, Rod Steiger, James Dean, Joanne Woodward and Lee Remick.

"Buffalo" Bob Smith originated the children's "Howdy Doody Show" in 1947 too, feeding the first generation to be brought up with television. Characters included the likes of "Clarabelle" – played by Bob Keeshan, who later became "Captain Kangaroo"

70

Facing page: "Buffalo" Bob Smith with puppet Howdy Doody and Muggs, the chimpanzee whose appearance on a news show during the coronation telecast in 1953 upset the British House of Commons.

Ventriloquist Paul Winchell and dummy Jerry Mahoney on ABC's "Circus" in 1956.

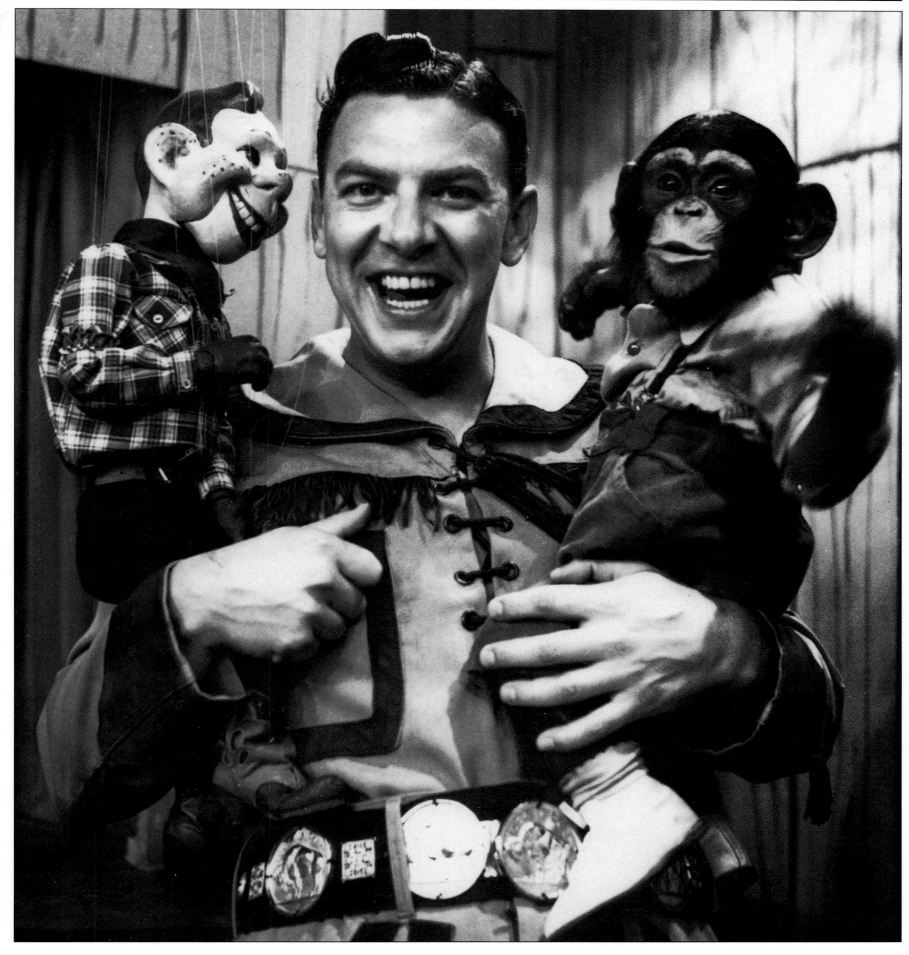

– "Princess Summerfall Winterspring" and "Chief Thunderthud."
This one-hour Saturday show on NBC was very popular throughout
its existence; tickets for the fifty seats in the studio's peanut gallery
("Doodyville") were hard to come by.

In Chicago, the local station WBKB started the children's show
"Kukla, Fran and Ollie," originally called "Junior Jamboree." The
hostess, Fran Allison, played along with Burr Tillstrom's puppets,
the "Kuklapolitan Players." These included Kukla (Russian for
"doll"), Ollie (Oliver J. Dragon to be precise), and Beulah the
Witch. (NBC picked it up for the network beginning January 12,
1949.)

Tillstrom once described it as "fortunate to begin in television
in the 'covered wagon' era. We grew along with the industry
itself." The puppets' popular show ran until 1957, later re-
appearing on public television and in syndication, finally going off
the air for good in 1976.

Facing page: Howdy Doody the puppet and Clarabell the clown checking photo entries for a competiton on the "Howdy Doody Show" in 1957.

73

The Burr Tillstrom puppets, Kukla and Ollie, together with Fran Allison, in a performance of "The Reluctant Dragon."

74

"Meet the Press" began a long-running television version of the public affairs program of the same name which had proven popular on radio. The format remained the same; a panel of reporters questioning a prominent public figure.

Faye Emerson had her own show in those early days, narrating a filmed fashion show from Paris. Her decolletage, daring for television then, provoked some complaints. At the beginning of 1948 there were still only one hundred and seventy-two thousand sets (with screens between seven and fourteen inches) and fewer than twenty television stations.

The fear of what television would do to attendance at the movies and sports events made for lively debate. But television's small budgets at the time made it a poor rival. Television was still the butt of jokes, still the runt of the communications litter dominated by radio.

Facing page: an early broadcast of "Meet the Press," which made its TV debut in 1947, hosted by Lawrence Spivak (standing) and featuring former president Herbert Hoover.

75

Faye Emerson's décolletage created a stir in the early days of television and put her among the ten best-dressed women in a 1950 opinion poll.

76

George Burns and Gracie Allen rehearsing in their Beverley Hills home in 1951.

(George Burns remembered doing a radio show with Gracie Allen in the late 1930s: "Maybe I'd better wait for television before I tell that joke again," he said.

"Oh, no, dear," came Gracie's reply, "television won't help you any."

It got a big laugh.)

It was 1948 before it became clear that this was to be the Age of Television. Manufacturers were selling more than two hundred thousand receivers a month, nine hundred and seventy-five thousand new sets were built during that year. There were some thirty stations in fifteen states by this time. The Washington, D.C., and New York *TV Guide* began publication, with a picture of

77

George and Gracie at the Stork Club in 1954.

Facing page: the young
Douglas Edwards, whose
"Douglas Edwards with the
News" was broadcast on
weekday evenings on CBS.

Gloria Swanson on its cover. At last there was something to see;
prime-time was now prime.

Popular radio programs like the "Major Bowes Amateur Hour"
(DuMont) and the debate program, "America's Town Meeting of
the Air" (ABC) followed "Meet the Press" to the newer medium.

News began to take its place in the picture.

Local news was an early staple of television; radio commentator
Lowell Thomas often simulcast his "Sonoco News" on New York
TV in 1940. Douglas Edwards was among several who had been
doing local news since the mid-1940s.

Edwards anchored the first nightly television news – "Douglas
Edwards … With the News," on CBS in 1948. It later became the
"CBS Evening News" with Walter Cronkite taking over as anchor.
The two men were among a number of fine journalists who had
worked with Edward R. Murrow's CBS Radio staff in London
toward the end of World War II. Other "Murrow's Boys" included
Eric Sevareid, Charles Collingswood, Howard K. Smith, Robert
Trout and Richard C. Hottelet.

Newsman Edward Murrow,
known to puff up quite a
smokescreen on the air.

Edwards had joined CBS Radio in 1942. He had previously held the post of Paris bureau chief for CBS and also taken part in the coverage of the presidential conventions of 1948. It was CBS News president Frank Stanton who tapped him for the television job.

Don Hewitt was associate producer and later producer of that first television newscast. (He was also to become creator and executive producer of "60 Minutes.") He recalled saying to a friend's suggestion that his experience at a newsphoto service might help in broadcasting:

"I said, 'what does CBS want with picture experience? Radio doesn't need any pictures.' He said, 'No ... television.' I said, 'What-a-vision?'"

Edwards, who retired in 1988 after forty-six years in broadcasting, remembered those early days: "CBS asked me to go into television and I did it with some fear and trepidation and trembling, not because I was nervous about being on television, I had done quite a bit of it [including the "Kukla, Fran and Ollie" show in Chicago], but radio was the power and I was pretty young at the time."

The CBS network then had half a dozen Eastern cities and every other night or so, Edwards recalled, he would welcome a new station to the hookup – until one night he was able to say, "Good evening, everybody, coast to coast."

NBC followed with its evening news show "Camel News Caravan" with John Cameron Swayze, sponsored by Camel

Facing page: each week Edward Murrow invited his viewers to join him in the homes of celebrities on "Person to Person."

Ted Husing, a sports announcer in the early days of radio.

cigarettes. ABC later began a nightly news show with John Daly.

Near the end of his show, Swayze would introduce a quick series of items for which there was no film, with the announcement that it was time for "hopscotching the world for headlines." He'd always finish by saying "That's the story, folks. Glad we could get together!"

Swayze would later be the commercial spokesman for Timex watches: "They take a lickin', but keep on tickin'."

It was also the beginning of an awareness among politicians that television was capable of bringing the voters to them. Both the Democrats and the Republicans chose to hold their 1948 nominating conventions in Philadelphia. This was because Philadelphia was on the coaxial cable link to major cities in the East and could be expected to reach a television audience of millions.

After Harry S. Truman was elected (Truman's inauguration was the first to be televised), David Sarnoff noted the significance. He predicted that Television would cause vast changes in political strategy and enable candidates to attain a more intimate contact with the voters.

"More Americans have seen President Truman by television in one evening than saw Lincoln during his entire term in the White House... In 1861, the population of this country numbered thirty-eight million. Today more than that number of people live within the areas already covered by television."

Charles E. Cropley (center), clerk of the Supreme Court, at President Harry Truman's inauguration ceremony in 1949. The picture is taken from an NBC television set in New York.

Television, he said, would enable candidates to transmit "their complete personalities" to the voters.

It was a grand and exciting time for the television baby and its viewers. Some were to call it the beginning of the "Golden Age of Television."

A look at TV listings for a typical week in 1948 showed a Sunday night lineup that included "Studio One," "Toast of the Town," "The Original Amateur Hour," "Meet the Press" and the "Philco Television Playhouse."

Monday night offered "Arthur Godfrey's Talent Scouts" and boxing from St. Nicholas Arena.

On Tuesday, streets emptied and neighbors gathered at the new hearth to see the "Texaco Star Theater" with Milton Berle –"Uncle Miltie," later to become "Mr. Television." There was also "America's Town Meeting of the Air;" boxing and wrestling.

Wednesday promised the "Kraft Television Theater" and more boxing and wrestling.

Facing page: Arthur Godfrey's trademark smile and ukulele on one of his shows in 1952.

Jackie Gleason encircled by the thirty-two dancers who featured on the weekly CBS show he modestly called a "tiny spectacular." The show made use of a fifth camera, used overhead to show off the geometric patterns made by the dancers.

85

86

The next day, viewers could "Face the Music" or face "The Bigelow Show," with ventriloquist Paul Winchell, dummy Jerry Mahoney and Dunninger the mental telepathist.

On Friday it was "Break the Bank," more wrestling and "Gillette's Cavalcade of Sports."

There were more sports on Saturday night, along with the country music show, "Saturday Night Jamboree."

At the end of 1948, NBC's David Sarnoff declared television two years ahead of the most optimistic predictions made at the end of the war:

"The accelerated progress has lifted radio and television, in combination as an industry, to a $2.5 billion-a-year enterprise. If the rate of growth continues as the market indices and public acceptance indicate it will, radio-television should rank as one of the ten foremost industries in the United States by 1953."

In January 1949, television extended the range of its vision from the Atlantic Ocean to the Mississippi River (halfway across the continent) with the joining of a new link between Philadelphia and Cleveland, Ohio. An Associated Press television writer, Arthur Edson, saw the hookup as "the beginning of the end of the American way of life as we know it."

More than half in jest, he wrote: "You doubt that this is an event of tremendous import?

"Well, no one paid much attention when Henry cranked his first Ford, either.

"But the automobile yanked us out of our homes. It made the city more accessible to the farmer than the general store had been. It turned the country into a potential playground for hemmed-in city dwellers. It drove us to faraway places we scarcely had dared to dream of seeing.

"Now television threatens to lure us back into our homes, and chain us there."

87

These pages: ventriloquist Edgar Bergen with sidekicks Charlie McCarthy and Mortimer P. Sherd, 1938.

Maybe, he suggested, these new viewers are pioneers, like the early radio crystal set owners, "who used to stumble into the office each morning after a hard night of trying to get Paducah on the wireless. In time, they outgrew it.

"But if television, in its infancy, has such a hold, what can we look forward to when it can fetch in the best from coast to coast?"

Viewers weren't the only ones concerned with the effects of the fledgling industry. Hollywood and motion-picture-theater owners, as well as sports arena operators, worried what it might do to their attendance.

The motion picture industry, from technicians to producers, began to take television seriously, wondering just how much business it was likely to take away from them. They wanted to

Red Skelton during a TV performance in 1952, the year in which he was awarded Emmys for Best Comedy Show and Best Comic.

88

know just where the movie house fitted into the public interest with this rapidly developing electronic "gadget" just come on the scene.

Wayne Coy, FCC chairman at the time, gave movie interests a pep talk:

"You are wondering who will stand in the queue buffeted by the wind, the rain and the snow to see your show when he can see all that without stirring from his easy chair. In the coming battle between celluloid and electronics, you theater men are going to give your customers a bigger money's worth than they have ever gotten before – pictures with better writing, better acting, better directing, better photography."

In retrospect, it was intriguing optimism.

Marlo Thomas with her toe stuck in a bowling ball in an episode of "That Girl" called "This Little Piggy had a Ball." Ted Bissell is trying to help.

89

Other opinions at the time ranged from doom to apathy; some said it would, as radio had, find its own place in the economy, with little appreciable effect on existing industries.

But there seemed little, if any, disagreement that the new "gadget" was here to stay and would be a success.

In 1949, one million TV sets were sold in the United States. The *Sears, Roebuck* catalog advertised television sets, "with indoor antenna," for $149.95 cash, or $15.50 down with $7 a month h.p.

CBS, under the new leadership of William C. Paley, had begun to lure popular radio comedians – like Jack Benny, Burns and Allen, Red Skelton and Edgar Bergen – from NBC. Among other attractions, CBS offered them a salary plan that would give them huge tax breaks.

The radio show "Candid Microphone" moved over to TV, continuing to set up practical jokes under the title "Candid Camera," with Allen Funt still producing and hosting.

Crime shows like "Man Against Crime," with Ralph Bellamy, started in 1949, followed by "Martin Kane, Private Eye" and "Mr. District Attorney."

The first "thriller" series, "Suspense," previously a fixture on CBS Radio, was first telecast on March 1, 1949, live from New York.

Facing page: Red Skelton and Mickey Rooney.

90

Employees at Fox Television monitoring the phones in the station's Washington studio after a broadcast of "America's Most Wanted," in which actors dramatized real crimes and appealed to the public for help in solving them.

A former vaudevillian, Milton Berle, began a variety show called the "Texaco Star Theater." "Uncle Miltie" (who had appeared before experimental TV cameras in Chicago in 1929) could clear a street on Tuesday nights at 8 p.m. more effectively than a wartime air raid drill. (One movie theater put a sign on the door: Closed Tuesday – I Want To See Berle, Too.)

Restaurants and movie theaters felt the pinch on Friday nights too when the "Admiral Broadway Revue" went on the air, teaming comedians Sid Caesar and Imogene Coca for the first time. Later, the pair were to be popular co-stars on "Show of Shows," with other comic talents including Carl Reiner and Howard Morris, with scripts by Neil Simon, Mel Brooks, and Woody Allen.

92

Milton Berle, in drag as Cleopatra and dressed as a football player.

94

Left: Sid Caesar, on "Caesar's Hour" in 1956.

Facing page: Sid Caesar and Imogen Coca in a scene from the successful series of comedy/variety skits "Your Show of Shows," which featured scripts by Mel Brooks, Woody Allen and Neil Simon.

Ed Sullivan, a columnist on New York's *Daily News*, was host of another variety show, "Toast of the Town," later to become "The Ed Sullivan Show," and dominate Sunday nights.

Sulivan's first show featured, among others, the comedy team of Dean Martin and Jerry Lewis. In the years to come, there was a seemingly endless list of stars, from Louis Armstrong and Pearl Bailey to Elvis Presley and the Beatles – in their first appearance in the United States. (Although Steve Allen had earlier "introduced" them on film during his show).

The Presley appearance made headlines. Because of complaints about the singer's rock style, with his gyrating hips, he was shown on TV only from the waist up.

Nanette Fabray chokes as Sid Caesar, Carl Reiner and Howard Morris puff their cigars over her in a commuting sketch on Caesar's show.

96

TV master of ceremonies Ed Sullivan, in 1955.

The Beatles' appearance really made history. On that February 9 show in 1964, the British rock group was billed along with the comedy team of Mitzi McCall and Charlie Brill, impressionist Frank Gorshin, a tumbling act called the Four Fays, and thirty-seven members of the cast from the Broadway musical, "Oliver." Sullivan, more animated than usual, handled the squealing audience as a father would a hyperactive child. He gently shushed them and made the girls promise to stay in their seats. After introducing a commercial for "Aero Shave," he swept his arm through the air as the curtain parted. The Beatles craze began in earnest.

Often teased for being "stone-faced," Sullivan would characteristically fold his arms to announce his lineup of guests, promising a "really, really big show" (which he pronounced "shew"). During the hour the former gossip columnist would point out the numerous celebrities in his audience.

Below: Ed Sullivan, bringing the "big shew" to CBS.

Right: the Beatles' debut on the Ed Sullivan Show, February 9, 1964.

("Ed Sullivan will last as long as other people have talent," Oscar Levant once said.)

Arthur Godfrey, the personable and folksy radio star, was welcomed to television as host of "Arthur Godfrey's Talent Scouts" and, very soon after, "Arthur Godfrey and His Friends." The "Ol' Redhead," as he was known, topped TV ratings for several years with both shows.

Godfrey was the "homey" performer; his stage set was our living room; his friends, our friends. Among these friends were the announcer Tony Marvin, singers Frank Parker and Marion

100

The Beatles with the folk singers Peter, Paul and Mary, in London with Ed Sullivan shortly after their debut on his show.

Arthur Godfrey with his ever-popular ukulele, 1958.

The McGuire sisters, (left to right) Chris, Phyllis and Dorothy, on Arthur Godfrey's show in the 1950s.

Marlowe, the McGuire sisters and Julius LaRosa. The show even featured an authentic family fight when a dispute with LaRosa ended with Godfrey firing his long-standing sidekick on the air.

These shows were live, as was "Roller Derby," an odd new sport that captured the interest, if not the imagination, of viewers. It involved teams of skaters racing around an oval track, scoring points by passing members of the opposite team – usually by knocking them over. Women like Midge "Toughie" Brasuhn and Gerry Murray seemed to do it best and were more popular than their male counterparts.

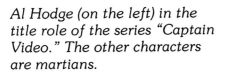

Al Hodge (on the left) in the title role of the series "Captain Video." The other characters are martians.

Captain Video introduced the "discotron" into his show in the 1950s. The futuristic machine was described as a "portable television set that can show any subject of interest to the operator, anywhere in the world."

The game show "Charades" was also popular at this time, with celebrity guests competing.

DuMont had success with the children's program, "Captain Video and the Video Rangers," from its start in June 1949 until the network left the air in 1955. Captain Video, "the guardian of the safety of the world," no less, was played by Richard Coogan and, later on, by Al Hodge (formerly the radio voice of "The Green Hornet"). There are still numerous "at-home Rangers" proud to show off their Captain Video decoder ring – one of many replicas offered as premiums during the run of the show.

Television was also showing theatrical movies, including the popular Westerns of "Hopalong Cassidy," starring William Boyd and his sidekick George "Gabby" Hayes. Boyd made a new series of films for TV with Edgar Buchanan, which ran on NBC from 1949. It was considered the first TV Western series.

The year 1949 began with radio still drawing a mighty eighty-one percent of the audience. At year's end TV had cut it down to fifty-nine percent.

Television was putting vaudeville, motion pictures, newsreels, musical comedy and sports events into the nation's living rooms.

Television had become very important. It was a strong rival to the popularity of radio. It had come into homes and into taverns, with live events, with news, with entertainment, with sports.

By 1950, it had become a necessity.

103

George "Gabby" Hayes, a onetime sidekick of Hopalong Cassidy, featured on NBC in 1951, spinning tales about his fictitious family and helping children learn American history through dramatized true stories.

Captain Video (Al Hodge) and his sidekick, Ranger (Don Hastings).

CHAPTER III

THE GOLDEN AGE

What made this television's Golden Age? Was it truly a unique time, a "golden" time, or is the epithet simply nostalgia for the "good old days," when life was simpler?

It was undeniably a shining era for television; it was when the medium came of age.

The imaginative and creative were able to work with somewhat of a blank screen. There were no cemented precedents as yet; everything seemed open for a try. High costs and other economic pressures were challenges, but still relatively minor obstacles to be overcome with a little ingenuity. Here was a fresh opportunity to communicate, to reach millions of people at once; with information; a message; a story.

The time was ripe, the young, upstart medium had now established itself as a serious contender for audiences. In 1950, during the months of March and April alone, one hundred and five thousand TV sets had been sold.

TV had cut sharply into radio listening figures and was beginning to grab movie audiences. Adult movie attendance was down a whopping seventy-two percent at the end of 1950.

Hollywood signs campaigned, only half in jest, to "Stamp Out TV." Eric Johnston of the Motion Picture Association of America said, "We will simply have to face the fact that we are in for a leveling off in the future because of the public's driving habits [drive-in theater business was up] and television." Movie-theater closings were no longer uncommon.

Most glistening and attracting in this Golden Age were TV's live drama anthologies. Live!

John Frankenheimer, who directed one hundred and forty live television shows on "Climax" and "Playhouse 90," once recalled for *American Film* magazine: "When I got into television in 1953, there was no such thing as magnetic tape. You had two forms of TV in those days. One was film television, which was done out in Hollywood. ... The other was live television. That was it. So, it wasn't a question of whether or not we wanted to do live television; that was the only thing there was."

The "live" aspect was a key part of what made those early television days exciting, though there were other facets. "The Golden Age was golden largely in the sense of opportunity," author Gore Vidal recalled in the book "Television," a companion

A battery of lights, cameras and sound equipment surrounded performers on an NBC studio shooting of the "Swift Variety Show" in 1948. Fifteen men, including cameramen, electricians, stagehands, engineers, producers and directors, were involved in the broadcast.

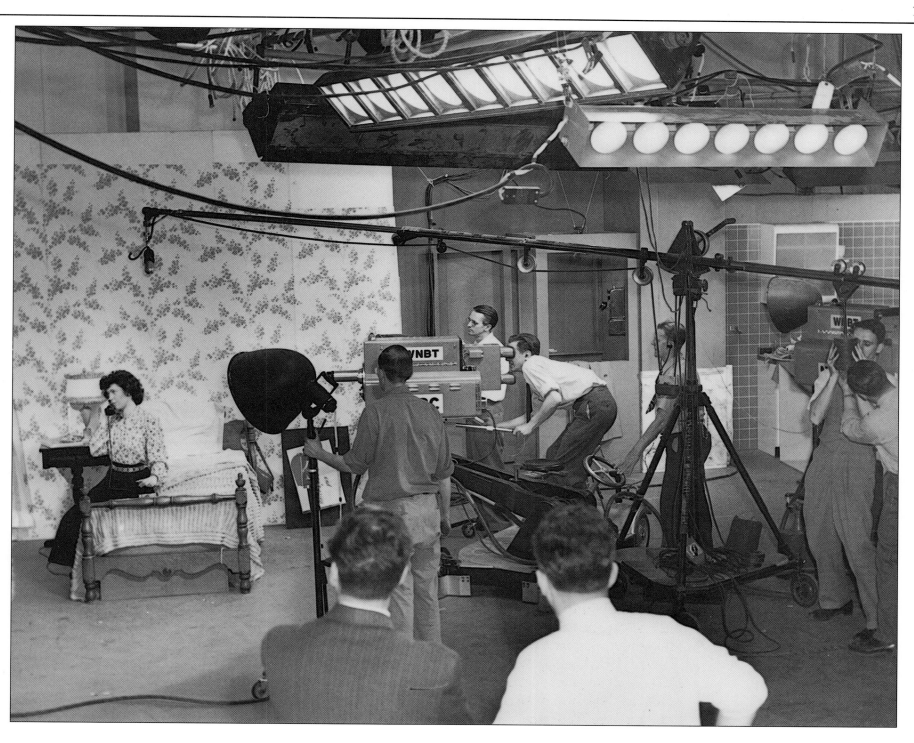

to the television series on the history of the medium. "There was an awful lot of drama. Television was still new and exciting.

"Everybody watched. You would walk down the street the next day and you would hear people talking about it. You had a sense of the audience, and you had a sense that what you did was needed."

Vidal was one of those contributing to the gold mine of live plays that were televised on those popular anthology series. Amongst these were "The Kraft Television Theatre," "Ford Theatre," "Playhouse 90," the "Philco TV Playhouse," "Goodyear TV Playhouse," "Studio One," "The Alcoa Hour" and "The U.S. Steel Hour."

The well-known Shakespearean actor Maurice Evans produced "Hallmark's Hall of Fame" for a 1955-56 season, with "Alice in Wonderland," "The Taming of the Shrew" and "The Corn Is Green" among the productions. "Our job," he said then, "is to lead public taste, not play to what is thought to be public taste."

A production of Hemingway's "For Whom the Bell Tolls," on "Playhouse 90" in 1959, directed by John Frankenheimer (on the right) and starring Jason Robards Jr. and Maria Schell. Shown in two parts, it was TV's first three-hour-long drama.

106

"Ford Theatre" began as a monthly series in 1948 and became a regular hour-long series a year later, shown every other Friday night on CBS. Then, after a year's absence, it returned on NBC with half-hour plays. Future President Ronald Reagan and his wife to be, Nancy Davis, made their first acting appearance together on "Ford Theatre," in a play called "First Born."

Among the extraordinary group of writers contributing were Paddy Chayefsky, Horton Foote, Reginald Rose and Rod Serling.

Outstanding original plays included Chayefsky's "Marty," Rose's "Twelve Angry Men," J.P. Miller's "The Days of Wine and Roses," William Gibson's "The Miracle Worker" and Serling's "Patterns" and "Requiem for a Heavyweight." (Serling would later create the "Twilight Zone" series.) The play "Marty" starred Rod Steiger but was later made into an Academy Award winning film with Ernest Borgnine. "Twelve Angry Men" also had success as a movie of course.

A list of just some of the actors in these productions reads like

A serviceman and his family enjoying television at the Air Force base in Limestone, Maine, in 1954.

a theatrical "Who's Who." Among them were Jack Palance, Cliff Robertson, Piper Laurie, Paul Newman, Mickey Rooney, Art Carney, Anthony Quinn, Grace Kelly and Jose Ferrer. In addition were Charlton Heston, Sidney Poitier, Rod Steiger, Eli Wallach, Tony Randall, Margaret Sullavan, Richard Kiley, John Forsythe and Joanne Woodward.

Many of them were Broadway actors who had taken the opportunity to get away from the roles they were playing eight times a week. Many were Actors Studio hopefuls. Most would go on to bright acting careers.

Movie actor Ronald Reagan began hosting a dramatic series called "General Electric Theater" on Sunday nights.

The dramas also gave opportunities to producers and directors,

108

Ronald Reagan and Diane Brewster with youngster Evelyn Rudie in "Nobody's Child," on "General Electric Theater" in 1959.

Bud Collyer (to the rear) was master of ceremonies on "To Tell the Truth," on which panelists in 1957 included (left to right) Polly Bergen, Ralph Bellamy, Kitty Carlisle and Hy Gardner.

Members of baseball's Oakland As and Los Angeles Dodgers, on the syndicated game show "Family Feud" in 1988.

including Fred Coe, John Frankenheimer, Arthur Penn and Sidney Lumet.

It was indeed a golden age for television.

Television images crossed the continent for the first time on September 4, 1951, with the televising of President Truman's address at the Japanese Peace Treaty Conference in San Francisco.

News accounts from New York reported: "The President could be seen as clearly on this end of the 3,000-mile hookup as if he had been speaking from the studios of a New York station, and probably better than from rear seats in the War Memorial Opera House where he delivered his address."

Estimates of the television audience for the first coast-to-coast TV hookup ranged upward from twenty million. The telecast went to fifty-four cities, covering an area with nearly thirteen million TV sets in use.

It was noted that this "historic first" came nearly twenty-five years after the start of transcontinental radio broadcasts on a substantial scale, and some thirty-six years after the inauguration of the coast-to-coast telephone service.

Two years later, the Coronation of Queen Elizabeth II was to mark the birth of international television, with BBC film shown on U.S. and Canadian stations. The U.S. networks used film of the BBC broadcast, developed and edited on a chartered DC-6 jet, and shown on U.S. stations the same day. Through the fledgling European TV network known as "Eurovision," live transmission

Facing page: Lou Babcock (on the right) on "This is Your Life" in 1953, hosted by Ralph Edwards (kneeling), with Lila Nuenfeldt and the show's director, Axel Gruenburg, himself one of Miss Babcock's former students.

Former Olympic swimmer Duke Kahanamoku starred on "This is Your Life" in 1957. Host Ralph Edwards is at left, with Olympic swimmers (left to right) Michael McDermott, Kahanamoku, Johnny Weissmuller and Ludy Langer.

112

Dave Garroway and Helen O'Connell on the set of the "Today" show in 1958.

of the coronation was carried as far as Berlin – by way of France, Holland and West Germany. Since three transmission standards were involved on the Continent, converters were set up in Paris and Breda, Holland.

It wouldn't be until 1959, though, that TV newsreel film was transmitted over the Atlantic by telephone cable. The mastering of that feat was on the occasion of the departure of Queen Elizabeth II and Prince Philip for Canada, to open the St. Lawrence Seaway. The film was broadcast on U.S. television less than two hours later, in a relay from Montreal, Canada. But it had been the Coronation that fulfilled the envisionment of the "front row seat" on world events promised by this new form of instant communication.

It became more apparent than ever that television was outgrowing its adolescence and had to take on the responsibilities of an adult medium.

Evidence of the more serious aspects of television was seen in documentary series such as March of Time's "Crusade in Europe" and "Victory at Sea" – and in the in-depth "See It Now," with host Edward R. Murrow.

Murrow had earned his considerable journalistic reputation on CBS Radio, with his wartime report, "This Is London." In 1948, he and Fred Friendly produced a "Hear It Now" album, recording the voices of history. As on-air correspondent of "See It Now," he took on controversial, and often unpopular, issues. He became America's most celebrated newscaster, however; a familiar figure with an ever-present cigarette in hand and a dramatic, staccato speaking voice.

113

Edward R. Murrow, working in England in 1959.

114

Barbara Eden, star of "I Dream of Jeannie."

The first broadcast of "See It Now," on a Sunday afternoon in 1951, reflected not only Murrow's sense of journalism, but also how far television had come technologically. Producer Fred Friendly recalled: "Edward R. Murrow and I were new to television. We were products of radio journalism. But we did know that we had this new instrument, and we wanted an opening that would be a statement of what we were trying to do."

The opening showed the Brooklyn Bridge and the Manhattan skyline on one side of the screen and the Golden Gate Bridge in San Francisco on the other.

"Here's the Atlantic; here's the Pacific Ocean," Murrow said. "We are impressed by a medium through which a man sitting in his living room has been able for the first time to look at two oceans at once."

In the years to follow, "See It Now" moved to Sunday nights, then Tuesday nights, and Murrow was to have many of the most important people of the day as guests. His interviews included President Truman on General Douglas MacArthur, Douglas MacArthur on President Truman, Soviet Premier Nikita Khrushchev, and Grandma Moses. He investigated the controversial case of J. Robert Oppenheimer, one of the creators of the atomic bomb, whose loyalty was subject to debate. The case of Lieutenant Milo Radulovich, an Air Force Reservist who had been asked to resign his commission because his family had been accused of "radical leanings," also featured on the show.

At the end of that show, Murrow said: "Whatever happens in

A robot serves breakfast to Mr Baxter (played by Don Defoe) and his family on "Hazel."

this whole area of the relationship between the individual and the state, we will do ourselves; it cannot be blamed on Malenkov, Mao Tse-tung, or even our allies. It seems to us – that is, to Fred Friendly and myself – that it is a subject that should be argued about endlessly."

That moving program was instrumental in getting the Air Force to decide Radulovich was not a security risk and allow him to retain his commission.

It was on "See It Now" that Murrow took on the powerful Senator Joseph McCarthy. McCarthy had been leading investigations into communist "subversion" in the State Department, the entertainment industry and the Army. With demagogic tactics, he had called many to answer before his special subcommittee, though their supposed affiliations were often based on innuendo and hearsay. Murrow spoke out:

"This is not the time for men who oppose Senator McCarthy's methods to keep silent. We can deny our heritage and our history,

116

Senator Joseph McCarthy being sworn in at the televised Congress-Army hearings investigating communist influence in 1954.

Lawrence Welk playing the accordion and leading his band to accompany "Champagne Lady" Alison Lon on the Saturday night program.

On "We the People," an early network show, farmer Herb Marlow (on the left) introduced his decoy pheasant to master of ceremonies Dan Seymour.

but we cannot escape responsibility for the result. There is no way for a citizen of a republic to abdicate his responsibilities.

"As a nation we have come into our full inheritance at a tender age. We proclaim ourselves – as indeed we are – the defenders of freedom, what's left of it, but we cannot defend freedom abroad by deserting it at home.

"The actions of the junior senator from Wisconsin have caused alarm and dismay amongst our allies abroad and given considerable comfort to our enemies, and whose fault is that? Not really his. He didn't create the situation of fear; he merely exploited it, and rather successfully. Cassius was right: 'The fault, dear Brutus, is not in our stars but in ourselves.'…"

He wrapped up with his trademark, "Good night … and good luck." It was not TV's first encounter with accusations of communist affiliations.

Early in 1950, a dancer named Paul Draper was invited to appear on Ed Sullivan's show. Draper had been the subject of a

118   *"Beat the Clock," a popular game show, involved slapstick stunts such as icing donuts, suspended from a rotating turntable on a man's head, with a soda syphon!*

letter-writing campaign naming him as a "pro-communist in sympathy." Sullivan and the Ford Motor Company sponsors resisted the pressures, but Draper found he could no longer earn a living in the United States and went to Europe.

An organization called "Aware" accused newsman John Henry Faulk of various "communist activities." CBS fired him. Years later, after numerous lawsuits, Faulk was exonerated and reinstated.

Philip Loeb, who co-starred with Gertrude Berg on "The Goldbergs," was similarly accused. He couldn't find any more work in the industry and eventually committed suicide.

The downfall of Senator McCarthy himself was witnessed by millions on television. The networks carried, either in full or in excerpts, the daytime Army-McCarthy hearings. The closeup exposure eventually resulted in a Senate censure of McCarthy.

CBS dropped "See It Now" in mid-1958, blaming high costs. Murrow later branched out to host "Person to Person" and made occasional appearances on "CBS Reports." In 1960, Murrow

Flipper in action on the '60s adventure series about two boys and their pet dolphin.

Walter Cronkite in Washington, 1972.

presented a documentary called "Harvest of Shame," a powerful program on the plight of the migrant worker in the United States – shown the day after Thanksgiving for extra effect. Documentary news lost a true champion when Murrow left the air. Many believe it never again reached the heights of pride, prestige and integrity that it had during those Murrow years.

Documentary news, of a sort (it was documentary drama, or what later proponents of the genre would call "docudrama"), was the feature of another programme, titled "You Are There." This show reenacted major events in history in a weekly series hosted by Walter Cronkite, who closed each show with:

"What kind of a day was it? A day like all other days, filled with those events that alter and illuminate our times. And you were there."

Cronkite, something of an heir to Murrow, was anchorman of CBS's Sunday news summary show from 1951. He took over the "CBS Evening News" in 1962 and was a highly-respected TV anchorman on the air for nearly twenty years.

TV newsmen in the '50s remained studio-bound; partly because jet travel and satellite technology were in their infant stages, and partly because TV equipment was still bulky and difficult to carry around.

Politicians, meanwhile, noted further evidence of the potential

Milton Berle (on the left), relaxing with producer and director Hal Kanter in 1958.

Jackie Gleason, as a "good-natured young loafer with money," starred with Betsy Palmer in the Pullitzer Prize winning play, "Time of Your Life," part of CBS's "Playhouse 90."

power of the small screen. Senator Estes Kefauver became a prominent national figure after the daytime televising of crime hearings from Washington.

In 1952 both Republicans and Democrats – aware that there were fifteen million TV sets in the United States by that time – agreed to televise their conventions. Sponsored by Westinghouse, the conventions made a household star of Betty Furness, who did the refrigerator commercials, live, throughout the events.

The Republicans hired an agency, Batten, Burton, Durstine & Osborne, to orchestrate Dwight D. Eisenhower's presidential election campaign against Adlai Stevenson. "Ike" won handily, despite some rough going for his vice presidential candidate, Richard Nixon.

Nixon had been questioned about his finances and he took to television to answer.

With his wife Pat at his side, Nixon spoke about a fund established by California supporters after his election to Congress, then added:

"One other thing I should probably tell you, because if I don't they'll probably be saying this about me too. We did get something – a gift – after the election. A man down in Texas heard Pat on the radio mention the fact that our two daughters would like to have a dog.

"And, believe it or not, the day before we left on this campaign trip we got a message from Union Station in Baltimore saying they had a package for us. We went down to get it. You know what it was? It was a little cocker spaniel dog in a crate that he sent all the way from Texas. Black and white spotted.

"And our little girl, Tricia, the six-year-old, named it Checkers. And you know the kids love that dog, and I just want to say this right now, that regardless of what they say about it, we're going to keep it."

Seven years after the "Checkers" speech, Nixon was to use television to his advantage again, this time in an encounter with Soviet Premier Nikita Khrushchev, at an exhibit in Moscow. The "kitchen debate" became the basis for his political reputation of being tough on the Communists.

Nixon was to have other key appearances on television; notably his broadcast debates with John F. Kennedy in 1960, when the results were not as pleasant for him. In 1972, his historic trip to China was covered on television.

Many years later, in retirement, Nixon was to tell *TV Guide:* "Of all the institutions arrayed with and against a president, none controls his fate more than television. Unless a president learns how to harness its power, his administration is in trouble from the beginning."

Television found myriad other ways to fill the hours – and show the commercials – during those "golden" years of the '50s.

122

Right: the control room of NBC's Color City in Burbank, California, opened in 1955. The monitors show a color test.

Below: a "Beat the Clock" stunt; the girl is attempting to transfer three eggs from the box into the spoons in her partner's mouth.

124

CBS's popular comedy and variety shows have included (facing page) "The Garry Moore Show" (top left), "My Three Sons" with Fred MacMurray (top right), "The Carol Burnett Show" (bottom left), and Ed Sullivan's "Toast of the Town" (bottom right), and (above) "The Danny Kaye Hour" (left) and "The Smothers Brothers' Comedy Hour" (right).

Everything from situation comedies, variety shows, public affairs programmes and game shows to cartoons, puppet shows, quizzes and Westerns, made their way onto the screen.

There were popular transfers from radio.

William Bendix had created the role of the lovable Chester A. Riley on "The Life of Riley" on radio, but when the program moved to television in October 1949, he was tied up making a movie. The role went to Jackie Gleason – his first TV series. Rosemary De Camp played his wife, Peg, and John Brown was the original Digby "Digger" O'Dell, the smiling undertaker. The show was canceled after one season, however, only to be revived in 1953 with Bendix, Marjorie Reynolds and Brown. The show's catch phrase caught the public imagination: "What a revoltin' development this is!"

Red Skelton was another radio émigré. He brought over his bag of characters; Mean Widdle Kid, Clem Kadiddlehopper and Willie Lump-Lump. He then added the hobo, Freddie the Freeloader. The comedy/variety program lasted twenty years.

The black characters of "Amos 'n' Andy" were played on radio by two white men, Freeman Gosden and Charles Correll (the shows producers.) When it moved to television in 1951, Amos and Andy were played by blacks Alvin Childress (Amos) and Spencer Williams Jr. (Andy), with Tim Moore as "The Kingfish." Because of some negative stereotypes – "Lightnin'" as the slow-moving janitor, for example – many complained it was racist. It ran just two years on CBS.

Jack Benny moved over to television, taking his underplayed style of comedy with him. Also with him went cohorts Eddie "Rochester" Anderson, Dennis Day, Mary Livingstone, and "Oh, Don" Wilson.

Yet another type of comedy, harder to describe, was introduced by Ernie Kovaks. Original and zany, visual and offbeat, Kovaks had as much fun experimenting with the visual trickery of television as he did with creating characters like Percy Dovetonsils and the Nairobi Trio.

Garry Moore (with Durwood Kirby and Carol Burnett) and "Lonesome George" Gobel had their own comedy/variety shows. "Four Star Revue" (later "All Star Revue") alternated hosts Ed Wynn, Jimmy Durante, Danny Thomas, Jack Carson, and later Martha Raye, George Jessel and Tallulah Bankhead.

Eddie Cantor served as one of the hosts of "The Colgate Comedy Hour." Fred Allen was another, but not for very long. He was one of the few top radio stars who couldn't seem to make the changeover to TV.

Another show generally fitting the musical/variety genre was "The Arthur Murray Party," which was once described as "the longest-running commercial in television history." Arthur and Kathryn Murray ran the Arthur Murray Dance Studio; her closing line each week was: "'Til then, to put a little fun in your life, try dancing."

The flamboyant pianist Liberace showed off his gilded and sequined fashions on his own musical variety show.

126

The incomparable Jimmy Durante.

Movie star Jane Russell on a 1955 episode of NBC's "Colgate Variety Hour," with players from baseball's Brooklyn Dodgers and New York Yankees. Standing (left to right): announcer Mel Allen, Hank Bauer, Duke Snider and Don Newcombe, crouching (from left): Yogi Berra, Pee Wee Reese and Carl Erskine.

"The Goldbergs" is considered by many to have been the first situation comedy on TV. It was the idea of Worthington Miner, then manager of television programming development at CBS. Miner had also created "Studio One," the children's show "Mr. I. Magination" (with Paul Tripp), and Ed Sullivan's "Toast of the Town."

Gertrude Berg had created the character of Mrs. Goldberg on radio. CBS brought the fictional middle-class Jewish family to television in January 1949. Mrs. Goldberg's ethnic "Yoo-hoo, Mrs. Bloom" to her Bronx neighbor, and her "Enter, whoever" reply to visitors at her door were familiar phrases to viewers for some six years.

Perhaps the most durable of the TV "sitcoms" was "Father Knows Best," which had begun on radio in 1949. CBS took it up in October 1954, only to lose it to NBC the next year. Reruns eventually played on both CBS and ABC networks.

It was the classic, wholesome family show, set in a "typical" Midwestern community with Robert Young (the only member of the radio cast who made it to the TV version) as patriarch of the Anderson family. Jane Wyatt played his TV wife in the series that was to set the standard for family situation comedies to come. Young later starred in "Marcus Welby, M.D." for seven seasons.

Another much-admired family comedy/drama hit TV audiences in 1949; "Mama," a series based on the Broadway play by John Van Druten. It was "I Remember Mama" on the stage, and many television viewers remember it that way as well. Each segment

127

Jasper, the part-afghan, part-collie star of "Bachelor Father," receiving a drink from Noreen Corcoran in 1958.

Carol Burnett doing her beloved characterization of a charwoman on "Carol & Company" in 1978.

128

began with a look at pages of a family photo album and a voice recalling, "I remember my brother Nels ... and my little sister Dagmar ... and of course, Papa. But most of all, I remember Mama."

It was the story of a Norwegian-American family, starring stage actress Peggy Wood in the title role, Judson Laird as papa, Rosemary Rice as daughter Katrin, and Dick Van Pattenson as son Nels. Dick Van Pattenson later became the patriarch of his own TV family in "Eight Is Enough". (Nels was one of Marlon Brando's first roles on Broadway.) It was popular enough to provoke audience complaints when CBS announced it was canceling the show in 1956 and was brought back for a brief run through March 1957.

In some ways, the program was the prototype of the family series of later years, "Ozzie and Harriet" and "Make Room for Daddy" (with Danny Thomas) among them.

At 9 o'clock on a Tuesday night in October 1950, a band started playing the "Love Nest" theme song – "The Burns and Allen Show" went on the air live from New York.

Burns introduced himself: "Hello, everybody, I'm George Burns, better known as Gracie Allen's husband. ..."

As Burns described it in his autobiographical "Gracie: A Love Story:"

"The interior of the house was decorated just like a real house in 1950 – we had no television set."

Facing page: the jewel in the crown of situation comedies on both TV and radio, "The Ozzie and Harriet Show," in its eighth year when this picture was taken in 1960. Ozzie is taking it easy with his real-life as well as on-screen family: sons David (left) and Ricky (right), and wife, Harriet.

129

Danny Kaye (on the right) plays a sour-faced waiter to Harvey Corman's chef in a sketch on CBS's "Danny Kaye Show" in 1966.

130

Jack Benny, Bing Crosby and George Burns rehearsing a takeoff of the old-time vaudeville team "Goldie Fields and Glide" for Benny's show in 1954.

Ed Wynn in 1952, celebrating his fiftieth year in show business, with Dinah Shore.

The innovative Ernie Kovacs, with Edie Adams.

The cast was the same as it was on radio: George Burns, Gracie Allen, announcer Bill Goodwin (to be followed by Harry Von Zell) and Hal March and Bea Benadaret, playing the neighbors Harry and Blanche Morton. Their son Ronnie joined the cast a couple of years later. John Brown, Fred Clark and Larry Keating followed March in the role of Harry Morton.

Two hundred and ninety-nine "Burns and Allen" shows ran over eight TV seasons, at first every other week live from New York, later filmed weekly. They did the final show on June 4, 1958, the last time Burns and Allen ever worked together. The last over the air "Say good night, Gracie" was on September 22, when Gracie retired because of a heart problem. At the time, it was the longest running situation comedy in television.

"I Love Lucy," which was the first television series to be filmed before a live studio audience, began on the night of Monday October 15, 1951, on CBS. It also pioneered the use of three cameras instead of one. Although most critics liked it, "I Love Lucy" was not an overnight ratings success, but it wasn't long before it became America's favorite. Within a year it was America's favorite situation comedy, with an estimated viewership of thirty-five million – second only to Red Skelton's show. As testament to its prime-time value, CBS gave the co-stars an $8 million, two year, no-cancellation contract in 1953.

The production was from Desilu, TV's first major independent studios, and featured Lucille Ball and her husband, Desi Arnaz, portraying Lucy and Ricky Ricardo, with Vivian Vance and Bill Frawley as Ethel and Fred Mertz.

Lucy and Desi and Ethel and Fred, like characters in so many other situation comedy series, became part of America's families, part of their neighborhood. They were so much a "part of the family" that when Lucille Ball became pregnant it was decided that the fictional Lucy would tell her "reel" – and real – husband on the air.

It went further: on January 19, 1953, Lucille Ball gave birth to a son, Desiderio Alberto Arnaz IV. That night, on television, Lucy gave birth to little Ricky and there was another member of the family-family.

Desi Jr.'s birth on television drew ninety-two percent of the television audience – larger than President Dwight D. Eisenhower's inauguration the next morning!

132

Below: Desi Arnaz at the wheel with Lucille Ball, Vivian Lance and William Frawley on the "I Love Lucy" show.

Facing page: Gale Gordon with Lucille Ball dressed as a movie stunt man on "The Lucy Show."

134

Above: Lucille Ball and Harpo Marx in "I Love Lucy."

Below: Ann Sothern and Don Porter in "The Ann Sothern Show."

Above: Maurice Gosfield and Phil Silvers in "The Phil Silvers Show."

"Beverley Hillbillies" Buddy Ebsen, Max Baer, Donna Douglas and Irene Ryan.

Above: Andy Griffith and Don Knotts in "The Andy Griffith Show."

Below: Gertrude Berg in "The Goldbergs."

Above: Bob Denver and Dwayne Hickman in "The Many Loves of Dobie Gillis."

Below: Mary Tyler Moore and Dick Van Dyke in "The Dick Van Dyke Show."

Weekly "I Love Lucy" shows became hour-long specials in 1957, and earlier episodes were sold for syndication. The various Lucy shows were seen in more than eighty countries. Lucille Ball remained on television for another twelve years after "I Love Lucy," with the weekly "Here's Lucy" and "The Lucy Show."

The redheaded Miss Ball, who died in 1989, is remembered not only for her comedic talents, but for a pioneering spirit that helped the fledgling television industry come of age.

The '50s burgeoned with family-oriented sitcoms, such as "Make Room for Daddy," and "Father Knows Best." Similarly, "Ozzie and Harriet" (with the real-life Nelsons: Ozzie, Harriet, David and Ricky) and, of course, "Leave It To Beaver" were also popular at this time. When "Leave It To Beaver" began, Beaver Cleaver was seven, his brother Wally, twelve. As they got older the stories developed until, in a final episode in 1963, Beaver (Jerry Mathers) was about to enter his teens and Wally (Tony Dow) was off to college. Among the more memorable characters was Eddie Haskell (Ken Osmond), overly polite to adults, but cruel to smaller kids.

A "Leave It To Beaver" revival in the 1980s led to the "New Leave It To Beaver" series, and a rerun of the 1957 pilot episode, which had a different cast than the regular one.

136

Singer Wayne Newton appearing as a guest on "The Lucy Show" in 1965.

"Leave it to Beaver" stars (from left to right) Tony Dow (Wally), Barbara Billingsley (June), Hugh Beaumont (Ward) and Jerry Mathers ("The Beav") left the air in 1963 but returned in reruns in the '80s.

One of the best-remembered of the situation comedies in this Golden Age had its roots in the variety show "Cavalcade of Stars" and its later entity, "The Jackie Gleason Show." It was in these shows that the characters of bus driver Ralph Kramden and his wife Alice took shape, along with their neighbor, Ed Norton the sewer-worker.

"The Honeymooners" went on the air October 1, 1955, and Gleason (Ralphie boy), Audrey Meadows (Alice), Art Carney (Norton) and Joyce Randolph (Trixie Norton) established their place in television history. Along with the show came the familiar lines: "To the moon, Alice ..." and, "One of these days, Alice ... one of these days ... Pow! right in the kisser!"

"The Honeymooners," one of the classic shows from the Golden Age of television, has survived because the live program was also recorded on film.

138

The original thirty-nine half-hour episodes have been syndicated, re-shown and re-run often since, along with the later shows.

Phil Silvers' situation comedy about Army life and Sergeant Bilko was originally called "You'll Never Get Rich," but that became the subtitle under "The Phil Silvers Show" just weeks after it premiered in September 1955.

"Duffy's Tavern" (... "Archie the manager speaking") had come over from radio, and "Mr. Peepers," a comedy series starring Wally Cox as a shy science teacher, appeared in 1952, the same year the police series "Dragnet" began.

One of the most successful police series ever on television, "Dragnet" starred Jack Webb as Sergeant Joe Friday in realistic

The Nortons and the Kramdens in "The Honeymooners."

139

140

Left: Sergeant Bilko (Phil Silvers), disguised as a British army officer, in a 1959 episode of the CBS show "You'll Never Get Rich" (later to become "The Phil Silvers Show"). Al Hodge is acting as foil.

Facing page: Jack Webb, star of "Dragnet," in 1956.

action that sharply contrasted with the situation comedies and variety shows of that decade. Sergeant Friday was a no-nonsense cop, and Webb's terse delivery of lines like "Just the facts, ma'am" and "My name's Friday; I'm a cop," caught on quickly among its viewers. The series lasted more than seven years in its original run.

From a child's point of view, television in the 1950s had much to offer.

Pre-schoolers found their niche with the "Ding Dong Schoolhouse" series in those days before "Sesame Street."

The success of "Kukla, Fran and Ollie" begat "Magic Cottage" and "Mr. I. Magination," while shows like "Captain Video," "Sky

Don Herbert and helper on "Mr Wizard," a weekly program shown on NBC from 1951 that introduced teenagers to science.

King," "Space Cadet" and "Captain Midnight" took another approach to attract a young audience.

"Wowee, kazowee, boys and girls" ... in January 1959, Bozo the Clown (Larry Harmon) took to the airwaves and has been seen there, somewhere, virtually every day since. He's "Bozo le Clown" in France, "Bozo el Payaso" in Brazil, and the longest-running live, daily children's television show in the United States. More than fifty thousand episodes have been produced, and some two hundred people have portrayed the snickering clown. Muppet-maker Jim Henson got some air time on Bozo shows and Big Bird, from "Sesame Street," is played by "Bozo Show" veteran Carroll Spinney.

Bob Keeshan as "Captain Kangaroo," who attracted more than eight-million viewers five mornings a week.

Among the better known children's shows of the time was "The Mickey Mouse Club," Disney's early entry into television. Viewer "members" knew the club song – M-I-C, K-E-Y, M-O-U-S-E ... – and Mickey Mouse ear caps were fashionable for a time. The daily variety show, on the air from 1955 to 1959, featured Jimmie Dodd as host and a talented young group known collectively as the "Mouseketeers." Annette Funicello was one of them.

For teenagers there was "The American Bandstand," or simply "Bandstand" as it was originally called when it hit the airwaves in September 1952. It was a WFIL-TV production from Philadelphia, with Bob Horn and Lee Stewart as hosts. Dick Clark, who became known as the Pied Piper of rock 'n' roll, took over the music and

Facing page: the Mouseketeers of the "Mickey Mouse Club," a daily children's show that started in 1955.

144

Mouseketeer Annette Funicello on Walt Disney's "Mickey Mouse Club" in 1975.

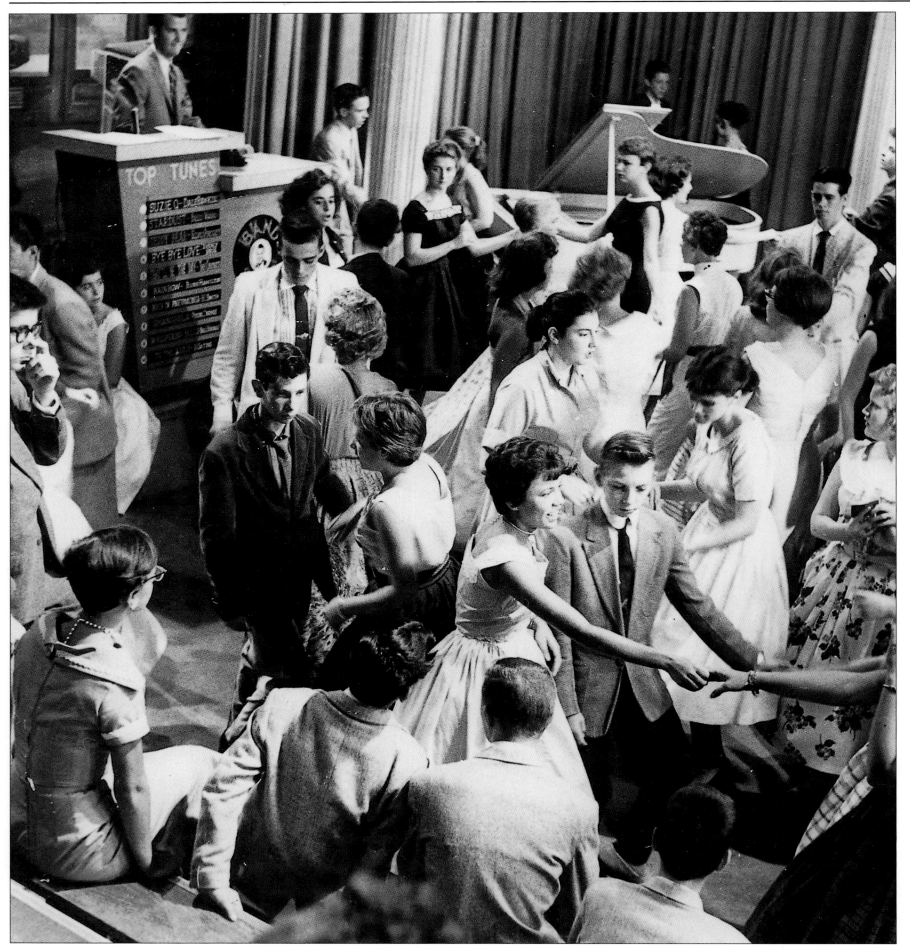

Facing page: disc jockey Dick Clark (on podium), surrounded by teenagers on his nationally televised dance show in 1958.

dance show in 1956. A year later it debuted on the ABC network. Clark was the host for thirty-three years ("Hey, hello there. Hey, welcome to 'American Bandstand'") before hanging up his saddle shoes as America's oldest teenager, "the squeaky-clean packager of pop."

During those years, in which the show became television's longest-lived variety program, "American Bandstand" introduced Stevie Wonder, the Jackson 5 and Madonna, as well as the bunny hop, twist and jerk dance crazes.

In 1952 the FCC set aside a number of channels specifically for education, though it made no provisions for financing them. The Ford Foundation made a grant to establish a production center, which came to be known as National Educational Television, and various university-related stations were set up, though few survived very long.

By 1956 only twenty-four non-commercial stations still existed, the strongest being those in New York, Boston, San Francisco and Pittsburgh.

The Ford Foundation considered adults, too; its TV-Radio Workshop funded the "Omnibus" series, hosted by the sophisticated Alistair Cooke. "Omnibus" had no commercial breaks – rare in commercial television. For four years it presented

Below: Art Carney, Jackie Gleason and Jane Meadows in "The Honeymooners."

Rehearsals for "The Many Loves of Dobie Gillis" in 1959. Tuesday Weld is playing opposite Dwayne Hickman as the first of his weekly dates.

opera, classical music, dance, dramatic plays and adventure films.

Bishop Fulton J. Sheen started out on the DuMont network in February 1952 with a show called "Life Is Worth Living." The popular religious series moved to ABC three years later and appeared opposite Milton Berle.

Berle, sponsored by Texaco, noted the new competition and said: "We both work for the same boss, Sky Chief."

Television was not only changing America's entertainment habits, but also its eating habits. The TV dinner – just pop it in the oven, it comes with its own aluminum tray – was introduced in 1954 and from then on cooking depended on the TV schedule for the evening.

TV also revised the nation's sleeping habits.

Early-hour viewers in 1952 got a first look at the "Today Show" with Dave Garroway, who previously had been host of "Garroway at Large" in Chicago. His "co-star," J. Fred Muggs, was a chimpanzee. The show became a hit when Muggs became a regular.

148

Jack Lescoulie (on the left) and Dave Garroway, chatting on the air, with "Today Girl" Florence Henderson in the background.

Right: Dave Garroway holding his co-host, J. Fred Muggs, on their morning "Today" show in 1953.

Above: (left to right) news editor Frank Blair, headman Dave Garroway, his right-hand man Jack Lescoulie and chimp J. Fred Muggs, posing for a photo on the second anniversary of the "Today" show in 1953.

Left: Frank Blair and Jack Lescoulie flank "Today Girl" Betsy Palmer on the set of the "Today" show in 1958.

150

The Jackson 5 appearing on "The Sonny and Cher Comedy Hour" on CBS in 1972.

The soap opera "Search for Tomorrow" made its debut on September 3, 1951, the first of its genre to be ultimately successful. "Big Sister" had aired in 1946 – for fifteen minutes – and "The First Hundred Years" aired for about one hundred days in 1950.

Soap operas had been enormously successful on radio since 1932 and "Clara, Lu 'n' Em." The move to television seemed natural. Larry Haines, an actor in "Search for Tomorrow," saw the similarities:

"In some ways a televised soap opera, while it concentrates on the visual, is like a radio soap opera. To be successful, it has to have good dialogue. You, the audience, must be able to hear the story. Seeing is not enough. The spoken word stimulates the imagination.

"For radio, it helps create a 'picture' in your mind. It also helps you 'see' more of the visual you're looking at on television.

"While TV has become more sophisticated and techniques are

151

Lee Aker as Rusty in the 1950s TV series "Rin Tin Tin."

brilliant, it's still the spoken word that's all-important."

Mary Stuart, also on "Search for Tomorrow," recalled in her autobiography what those early TV days were like:

"We were, to a great extent, in blackness. Because of the way the lights and the cameras had to operate at that time, black walls, black surroundings were necessary.

"Also, we were a live show. Therefore, we moved around as little as possible. Anything could happen on a live show, and usually did. So we did our best to minimize the risks wherever possible."

The themes of the soaps may have changed over the years, but the programs go on, to the delight of their followers. Most soap opera devotees are women. Among the millions who watch are an estimated three million who view the shows at their place of work during the day.

At the other end of the day, "Broadway Open House" began on May 29, 1950. The granddaddy of the informal talk show, it

was the idea of NBC's Sylvester "Pat" Weaver. Weaver had come to the network from the advertising agency of Young & Rubicam, to lure small-time advertising clients into the late-night viewing time. With Jerry Lester and his busty "sidekick" Dagmar and Morey Amsterdam as alternate emcees, along with Milton DeLugg as orchestra leader ("Orange Colored Sky"), the show was popular despite the hour. In August 1951 it became "The Steve Allen Show," appearing only on NBC's New York outlet until September 1954, when the name was again changed, becoming "Tonight" with Steve Allen as host.

Eventually, this kind of freewheeling comedy/variety/talk show became one of the most popular and successful program format on television. "The Tonight Show" with Jack Paar begun in 1957, and Johnny Carson followed suit in 1962. Carson remains a favorite of viewers today, beating more than a score of rivals, including Alan Thicke and Joan Rivers, with a show that is the longest-running series in television.

Facing page: Steve Allen wandering through his New York studio audience, which he called "The Snakepit," on his show "Tonight."

153

The wedding between Tiny Tim and Vicky Budginger was a memorable event on Johnny Carson's "Tonight" show in 1969.

154

Above: Groucho Marx on the game show "You Bet Your Life," with announcer George Fennman, and (above right) an amorous contestant in 1953.

Right: George Burns enjoying a dance at the age of eighty-five, on Dick Clark's "American Bandstand" in 1981.

Nor were game shows lacking in this period of television growth.

A most popular one was "You Bet Your Life," with Groucho Marx as host and George Fenneman as announcer – and a toy duck in a featured role.

The longest-running game show in prime-time network television was "What's My Line," which ran for eighteen seasons from 1950. John Daly was moderator, with a clever and engaging panel that included Arlene Francis, Dorothy Kilgallen, Bennet Cerf and Steve Allen.

Faye Emerson - *Radio Daily's* Woman of the Year for 1950 – seemed to be on every panel show going, including "I've Got a Secret" (1952), "Quick as a Flash" (1953), "What's in a Word" (1954) and "Masquerade Party" (1958).

Tom Poston (wearing the hat) whispering to Garry Moore as panelists Betsy Palmer (on the left) and Bess Myerson pretend to eavesdrop on "I've Got a Secret" in 1961.

155

Quiz show popularity reached a peak in 1954-5, lead by "$64,000 Question," a somewhat inflated version of radio's $64 Question." Others included "Twenty-One," "The Big Surprise," "Stop the Music," "Name That Tune," "Place the Face" and "The $64,000 Challenge."

Then, scandal rocked the industry and the nation both: quiz program corruption. A top quiz show winner, Charles Van Doren, admitted to having "deceived my friends, and I had millions of them." He told of irregularities, including knowing the questions and answers in advance. The networks dropped the big prize quiz programs, temporarily.

Soon after, Van Doren and thirteen others were indicted for perjury. There were later confessions of TV fraud in disc jockey

Facing page: Redmond O'Hanlon and his wife Marguerite, showing off a check for $16,000 which they won on the game show "The $64,000 Question" in 1955.

One revelation of the TV quiz show scandal that broke in 1959 was that the expressive contest between Charles Van Doren (top) and Herbert Stempel (bottom), on "Twenty One" in December 1956, was all an act.

"Gunsmoke" featured Marshall Matt Dillon, played by William Conrad (top left) on radio, and by James Arness (bottom left) on TV. Center: (top to bottom) Dennis Weaver as Chester, Milburn Stone as Doc and Amanda Blake as Kitty. Top right: Burt Reynolds (seated) played Quince and Ken Curtis (on the right) Festus Haggen. Bottom right: the cast.

158

"payola," the use of records in which disc jockeys had some financial interest. That "scandal" died out quickly.

Motion picture companies and agencies began to find it was more profitable to join television than to fight it, and several made deals to produce "telefilms." By the end of 1957, there were more than one hundred series of these TV films. They were generally westerns, which were just right for Hollywood's open spaces and back lots. While this was one of the reasons for the demise of live dramas on TV, it did provide viewers with new and exciting characters. Amongst these were; "Cheyenne" (Clint Walker), "Maverick" (James Garner), "Colt 45," "Lawman" and "The Rebel." "Wyatt Earp" (Hugh O'Brian), "Gunsmoke" (James Arness) and "Death Valley Days" followed later. "Bonanza"

James Arness (on the right) as Marshall Matt Dillon, with Dennis Weaver as his deputy, Chester, in the second season of "Gunsmoke," 1956.

160

Roy Rogers and Trigger saluting the audience for TV's "Roy Rogers' Championship Rodeo" in San Antonio, Texas, in 1955.

began in 1959, when there were thirty western series available during the prime-time viewing hours.

"Gunsmoke" was especially popular, and important in that it began a stampede of "adult westerns" that were to virtually take over television for the next decade. "Gunsmoke" began in 1955, a television version of the CBS radio show that had William Conrad (later of TV's "Cannon" and "Jake and the Fat Man") as Marshall Matt Dillon of Dodge City. James Arness played the role on the TV show, which began as a half-hour series, then went to a full hour on Saturday nights and ran for twenty years.

"Bonanza" was set on the Ponderosa ranch in Nevada in post Civil War days. The Cartwright family starred Lorne Greene as

James Arness as Marshall Matt Dillon in "Gunsmoke."

The Cartwright family, owners of the Ponderosa Ranch and stars of "Bonanza," the memorable theme tune of which helped make the show a big success.

the father, Ben, Michael Landon as Little Joe, Dan Blocker as "Hoss" and Pernell Roberts as Adam.

Somewhat akin to the Westerns were "animal" series, such as the ever-popular "Lassie," which began in 1957, and "My Friend Flicka."

The proliferation of western "shoot-'em-ups" and realistic police story telefilms appearing on home screens – including "The Untouchables," "77 Sunset Strip" and "Hawaiian Eye" – provoked some controversy. There was fear for their effects on juvenile crime and violence in general. Senators of both Tennessee and Connecticut, (respectively Estes Kefauver and Thomas Dodd) were leaders in rapping TV crime and violence. They pointed at "The Untouchables" series, that began late in October 1959, as perhaps the most violent show on television. Both led investigations and held hearings on the matter, but the debate continued unresolved.

Viewers and producers alike were beginning to see what a voracious appetite the tube had. It was eating up time, talent and program ideas as fast as the television set could be switched on.

162

The series "My Friend Flicka" was based on the book by Mary O'Hara, and starred (from left to right) Gene Evans, Johnny Washbrook and Anita Louise.

Lassie and John Provost in 1960.

Chapter IV

The Coming of Age

Newton Minow was a soft-spoken, good-humored thirty-four-year-old when he was named chairman of the FCC. A former Army Signal Corps sergeant, he said he preferred informational and educational types of programming – "but I like everything."

He made headlines in 1961 when he addressed the National Association of Broadcasters' convention and described television's program output as a "vast wasteland" that presented violence and mediocrity.

One day of programming, from sign-on to sign-off, he said, contained "a procession of game shows, violence, audience participation shows, formula comedies about totally unbelievable families, blood and thunder, mayhem, violence, sadism, murder, western bad men, western good men, private eyes, gangsters, more violence, and cartoons.

"And, endlessly, commercials – many screaming, cajoling and offending.

"And, most of all, boredom.

"True, you will see a few things that you will enjoy. But they will be very, very few. And if you think I exaggerate, try it."

He looked at the next planned season on television:

"Of seventy-three-and-one-half hours of prime evening time, the networks have tentatively scheduled fifty-nine hours to categories of action adeventure, situation comedy, variety, quiz and movies.

"Gentlemen, your trust accounting with your beneficiaries is overdue. Never have so few owed so much to so many."

What were the reasons? he asked rhetorically, and answered:

"Demands of your advertisers; competition for ever-higher ratings; the need always to attract a mass audience; the high cost of television programs; the insatiable appetite for progamming materials – these are some of them. Unquestionably, these are tough problems not susceptible to easy answers.

"But I am not convinced that you have tried hard enough to solve them."

His criticism was devastating, and he was not alone.

John Mason Brown had called TV "chewing gum for the eyes."

Newspaper columnist Harriet Van Horne had written: "There are days when any electrical appliance in the house, including the vacuum cleaner, seem to offer more entertainment possibilities

"College Bowl," one of numerous '60s quiz shows, pitted teams of university students against each other.

Right: hypnotist Arthur Ellen putting the spell on contestant Pat Morris on the "Truth or Consequences" TV show in 1955.

166

Below: Nanette Fabray steps over Sid Caesar in a lampoon of train commuting on "Show of Shows" in 1955.

Below: Nat Hinken (on the right) directing "Car 54, Where Are You?" in its first season in 1961, a show which he also wrote and produced. Joe E. Ross was the cop and Mickey Rich directed.

than the TV set."

She was later to describe her role as television critic as "one who roams the channels after dark, searching for buried treasure."

Yet, as Orson Welles was to admit, "I hate television. I hate it as much as peanuts. But I can't stop eating peanuts."

Indeed, America was hooked; it couldn't – or wouldn't – stop watching television. Forty million American families – eighty-eight percent of the whole - owned at least one television set by 1960; that's a hundred million viewers or more. There were fifty-six million TV sets in the United States in 1963.

Program and network executives searched for material to feed the hungry beast, to supply the increasing demand from viewers and sponsors.

Feature movies had provided much of the nourishment. These were mainly early westerns, films imported from England and low-budget features; the kind that were second billing at local theaters. Some independent stations went after quality features in the late 1940s and early 1950s, many of those British imports as well. When the networks finally put feature films on their program lists, they were all pre-1948 – Hollywood wasn't about to give quality features to its arch-rival.

167

Master of Ceremonies Jack Bailey and contestants having a ball on "Bathing Queen for a Day."

168

Comedy duo Elaine May and Mike Nichols became well known after their appearances on "The Jack Paar Show" in the '60's.

But on September 23, 1961, NBC showed "How to Marry a Millionaire," with Marilyn Monroe, Lauren Bacall and Betty Grable. It was part of a new series, "Saturday Night at the Movies." The films in the series were quality features made after 1948 – and Hollywood quickly became a major supplier for the small screen.

By the end of the decade there were as many as nine network movies on each week. Hollywood and TV were wedded in an arrangement that also produced the first of the made-for-TV movies, "See How They Run," in 1964. Many of the films were edited for television – for sex, bad language, violence and any sort of material network censors thought might prove offensive in a "family" medium.

Television had come a long way from the early days of controversy over Faye Emerson's plunging neckline and the use of the word "pregnant." Traditions of family entertainment remained solid, however, despite the permissiveness of the '60s decade. The bawdy "Tom Jones," and "Never on Sunday," a lighthearted story of a prostitute, were allowed on TV – though edited. Actor Rod Steiger remembered making "The Sergeant" in two versions – one for television and one for (presumably more liberal) movie audiences.

169

Marlon Perkins with an alligator on his wildlife-travel series "The Wild Kingdom."

Ron Ely as TV's "Tarzan" in 1960.

These pages: the many faces of Ernie Kovacs, a major influence in TV comedy, from his series in the 1950s.

Most popular, or at least highest-rated during the 1960s, were Alfred Hitchcock's "The Birds," "The Bridge on the River Kwai," and a rerun of "The Wizard of Oz." Later favorites were topped by "Gone With the Wind," "Airport," "Love Story," "Jaws" and "The Godfather."

But the movies, though they did end the war between TV and Hollywood, weren't enough. Nor did they appease those who had always seen television as a more edifying medium – a teacher more than an entertainer or baby-sitter.

There was some noncommercial television that attempted to provide that kind of material, launched through National Educational Television (NET) in 1952 with money from the Ford Foundation. But its programming was relegated to UHF (ultra-high frequency) channels, not available to a great number of viewers. By the mid-1950s only twenty or so noncommercial stations survived.

The Ford Foundation had also given funding to commercial television to provide more quality material. It had led to such series as "Omnibus," with Alistair Cooke as host, offering more cultural fare for Sunday afternoons.

Facing page: stars of the "Amos 'n' Andy" series on CBS in 1951: Tim Moore (top) as Kingfish, Spencer Williams (left) as Andy and Alvin Childress as Amos.

172

Donna Reed and co-star Carl Betz in the light comedy, "The Donna Reed Show."

In 1967, the Ford Foundation once again provided the monetary means ($10 million), this time for a Public Broadcasting Laboratory to produce a series of programs for educational stations. Its first offering was "Day of Absence," an off-Broadway play by Douglas Turner Ward.

Just days after the debut of PBL, the Corporation for Public Broadcasting was set up by federal law to promote non commercial television.

Commercial television wasn't exactly going out of its way to provide educational programming, and surveys showed a noticeable diminishment of its viewing among the more educated.

Had television so far been a "wasteland"? For those who had envisioned it as the ultimate teacher, the technological opportunity to expand knowledge and experience, there was a strong argument in agreement.

But the circumstances of life in the decade that was to become known as the "Turbulent '60s" was about to provide television with an opportunity to show what it could do best. It was to come in the realm of news, most often tragic news, solidifying the medium as the messenger, the home window on the world, the place to go to find out what was going on.

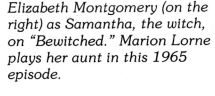

Facing page: (left to right) John Chancellor, Frank Blair and Ed Newman, on "The Today Show" in 1961.

Elizabeth Montgomery (on the right) as Samantha, the witch, on "Bewitched." Marion Lorne plays her aunt in this 1965 episode.

Below: Eva Gabor sharing the set of "Green Acres" with co-stars from the farmyard in 1967.

There was much of significance going on: a presidential campaign, a presidential assassination, civil rights riots, two more assassinations of national leaders – all under the glare and gaze of television cameras.

When John F. Kennedy sought the presidential nomination on the Democratic Party ticket, he turned to television and challenged Republican nominee Richard M. Nixon to public debates on the tube. They agreed to a series of four such debates in the campaign fall of 1960.

The first, held in a Chicago studio on September 26, was disastrous for Nixon, and it had nothing to do with the issues; it was simply how he was perceived on the screen. In Kennedy, television audiences sensed a confident air; he listened attentively and spoke crisply. In Nixon, viewers saw a fearful, haggard face, at times a perspiring one. To those who only heard the debate it seemed a fairly even match, to those who watched it Nixon was a clear loser.

It was a reaction not lost on political analysts, or, apparently, on the vast number of viewers – the Great Debates were seen by between sixty-one million and seventy-five million people. Many believe it made the difference in the election, eventually won by Kennedy by a narrow popular vote margin. Kennedy himself once said: "We wouldn't have had a prayer without that gadget."

As President, Kennedy made excellent use of television to communicate. In October 1962, for example, he asked for television time on all networks and went on the air to tell the public directly of the confrontation with Soviet Premier Khrushchev over missile sites in Cuba. He announced a "quarantine" of the island, in effect an ultimatum to the Soviets via television.

"I call upon Chairman Khrushchev to halt and eliminate this clandestine, reckless, and provocative threat to world peace and to stable relations between our two nations."

177

Facing page: Fred Astaire and dance partner Barrie Chase on "An evening with Fred Astaire" in 1958.

"Today" stars (left to right) Jane Pauley, John Palmer, Bryant Gumbel, Gene Shalit and Willard Scott.

178

Soviet leader Nikita Kruschev, interviewed by Stuart Novins for a tape-recorded appearance on "Face the Nation" in 1957.

It was effective – largely due to television's solidifying, or swaying, effect upon world public opinion.

It was a triumph for Kennedy – soon to be followed by tragedy.

At 1 p.m. on November 22, 1963, the soap opera "As the World Turns" was on the air.

It was interrupted by Walter Cronkite: "Here is a bulletin from CBS News."

It was the beginning of fifty-six hours of CBS transmission, covering the assassination of President Kennedy, the shooting of Lee Harvey Oswald and the Kennedy funeral.

After the initial bulletin, CBS returned briefly to regular programming – a commercial for Nescafe coffee – then Cronkite re-appeared on camera in the newsroom. There were live pictures from the Dallas Trade Mart, the site of a luncheon that was to have been the next stop on Kennedy's agenda on his campaign trip to Dallas, Texas. Eddie Barker of the CBS local affiliate KRLD passed on unconfirmed reports that the President was dead. The camera zoomed in on a weeping black waiter and later on workers sadly removing the presidential seal from the podium.

Dan Rather, working the story from KRLD by phone to the New York studio, confirmed the report of the president's death. Cronkite reported Rather's confirmation, although the official announcement did not come for seventeen more minutes.

Cronkite was handed a piece of news service copy: "From Dallas, Texas, the flash, apparently official," he said solemnly. "President .. Kennedy ... died at 1 p.m. Central Standard Time. Two o'clock Eastern Standard time." He took off his glasses and looked at the clock. "Some thirty-eight minutes ago." His voice cracked and he took a moment to collect himself before continuing.

"This one really struck home," he later recalled. "This was tearing the guts out. It was when you finally had to say the word, officially, that he was dead that it really impacted in the way it did."

179

180

Cronkite was on the air six straight hours.

NBC correspondent Bill Ryan was preparing the 2 p.m. network radio newscast when someone burst into his office, shouting: "Get back to TV right away! The president's been shot!"

It was 1:45 p.m. and NBC was due to transmit its daily noon-to-two break for local affiliates. Technicians had to rig a patchwork network of telephone lines before NBC could tell the nation that President Kennedy was dead. There were no satellite linkups, no microwave relays, no instant live pictures.

Ryan and Chet Huntley scrambled not only to report the news, but also to learn it, reading from Associated Press bulletins fed to them by technicians crouched at their feet.

A phone patch to NBC correspondent Robert MacNeil at Parkland Hospital in Dallas failed because of overloaded circuits. Anchorman Frank McGee, phone to his ear, passed along news from MacNeil bit by bit. A medical student kept the line open when MacNeil left the phone to learn fresh news.

There was no videotape, no film. Instead, Ryan held up AP Wirephotos of the motorcade through Dallas as Huntley recalled the days eighteen years earlier when President Roosevelt had died.

Ryan read the AP flash that Kennedy was dead.

"It's jarring," Ryan recalled later, "when somebody comes up to you and says, 'You're the one who told me President Kennedy was dead.' But a couple of people have phrased it exactly that way."

"The Donna Reed Show" family.

On Sunday, the networks were covering the movement of accused assassin Lee Harvey Oswald from the Dallas city jail to the county jail. Only NBC was on live when Jack Ruby stepped out of the crowd and shot Oswald point-blank. Tom Pettit was the correspondent at the scene:

"I clearly saw the shooting which was about six feet from where I was," he remembered. "I had a clear visual field to see somebody fire a revolver into Oswald's lower abdomen. I did not see Jack Ruby come through the crowd. I did not see anybody; I just saw the gunshot.

"What I was seeing was coming out of my mouth. It was the only time I've really experienced doing eyewitness reporting while you're live on the air."

Looking back, he said: "You know, it's a kind of a historic event in broadcasting, the first televised murder, but for me it was so horrendous a situation to be in and so emotional and so charged with fear, concern and a sense of pending doom that I would not like to relive it.

"I remember hearing our coverage when they had the casket at the rotunda of the Capitol. No narration, just symphonic music. Television really distinguished itself in that time, I think, really devoted itself to the notion that it was holding the country together, whether it was in truth or not, who am I to say? But at the time, we certainly felt that responsibility."

"It was a major moment of course in our history and in our television history," Cronkite was to say later.

181

Co-anchors of "NBC Nightly News" in 1982; Tom Brokaw (left) and Roger Mudd (right).

"I think we responded as an industry well. We showed our capabilities technologically and substantively as well – what we covered, how we covered it, the decorum with which we approached the story."

"I think these four days were the beginning for television journalism," Rather said. "There was a second-class citizenry to being a television journalist. That day, not only did we take you there, television journalists did some real good reporting.

"That day, we began to feel, 'Hey, we're as good as anybody.'"

Television was totally involved in that one story for four days; there were no network commercials from that Friday until the following Monday.

182

183

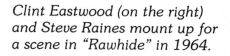

*Clint Eastwood (on the right)
and Steve Raines mount up for
a scene in "Rawhide" in 1964.*

One survey showed that ninety-six percent of the nation's households watched assassination news that weekend. The three networks carried more than forty-one hours of coverage; the average viewer watched for thirty-two hours – nearly nine hours a day – from the time of the assassination to the burial of the body.

America – and television – would never be the same.

Until the day the President died, the networks had been poor cousins to radio and newspapers in dispatching news to the nation. Nightly newscasts were only fifteen minutes long and news specials were reserved for things like space launches.

The assassination created a new hunger for TV news and brought television to the forefront of information carrying. CBS's

"Evening News" increased its nightly news show to half an hour in 1963. NBC did the same. The networks used much of the extra time to show Americans what was going on in a war halfway around the world, in Vietnam.

In the 1964 presidential campaign, Ronald Reagan made a televised speech for Senator Barry Goldwater, the Republican candidate. Reagan had already established a reputation as a crusader for conservative causes by touring the country with political messages as a spokesman for General Electric. He didn't help Goldwater in the long run, however, but surely bolstered his own reputation as a communicator who knew how to use television to his best advantage.

184

John Cameron Swayze in a pose familiar to viewers of NBC's "News Caravan" since 1948.

The fascination with the current events of the time also made celebrities of the messengers.

Howard K. Smith, after twenty years with CBS News, moved over to rival firm ABC to present a weekly news and commentary program. This show featured a summary of the week's major news events and interviews with the newsmakers. Smith paired with Harry Reasoner (also transferred from CBS) in December 1970 for a five year partnership when the show became "The ABC Evening News." Reasoner then took over alone.

In 1976, amid much hoopla, Reasoner was joined by Barbara Walters (formerly with NBC), who was reported to have been paid $1 million a year to make the switch.

The "60 Minutes" team: (standing, left to right) Harry Reasoner, Ed Bradley, Diane Sawyer, Morley Safer and (seated) Mike Wallace.

186

Jay Ward's TV cartoon characters included (from left to right) Rocky, Bullwinkle J. Moose, Boris Badenov and Natasha Fatale.

The news team of Chet Huntley and David Brinkley, which became popular during coverage of the presidential conventions, replaced John Cameron Swayze on NBC's nightly news. The "Huntley-Brinkley News Show" became something of a national institution, lasting almost fourteen years from its debut in 1956. Their habitual sign off, "Good night, Chet. ... Good night, David," became a popular phrase, replacing Swayze's "Glad we could get together."

Along with Walter Cronkite, Huntley and Brinkley were the first of the superstar TV newsmen, establishing anchormen as prestigious celebrities in their own right. As networks relied more and more on newscasts for revenue in the ensuing years, news anchors jumped from one network ship to another, lured more by top-scale salaries, it seemed, than prestige.

Newton Minow's "wasteland" began to blossom with something for everyone in the '60s.

"The Flintstones" children's cartoon series by William Hanna

Facing page: Ed Wynn in character as the "Perfect Fool" for the 1957 "Texaco Command Appearance."

188

Carl Reiner (on the left) and
Dick Van Dyke in a skit called
"The Gunslinger" on "The
Dick Van Dyke Show" in
1966.

Rosemary gets coquettish on
"The Dick Van Dyke Show" in
1962, with (from left to right)
Dick Van Dyke, Richard
Deacon and Morey
Amsterdam.

and Joseph Barbera started on September 30, 1960 and became the longest-running animated series in prime-time. Its spinoffs still fill Saturday morning hours.

Set in the Stone Age, the program featured the Flintstone family – Fred, Wilma and Pebbles, their pet dinosaur named "Dino" and their neighbors, the Rubbles – Barney, Betty and Bamm Bamm.

A futuristic counterpart to "The Flintstones," "The Jetsons" (also from Hanna-Barbera) only ran from 1963-1964, but developed a loyal following. George O'Hanlon was the voice of George Jetson, the cartoon world's man of the 21st century. O'Hanlon had unsuccessfully auditioned for the role of Fred Flintstone (Alan Reed got the part).

"George Jetson was an average man. He has trouble with his boss, he has problems with his kids, and so on," O'Hanlon once said. "The only difference is that he lives in the next century."

In 1985, forty-one new episodes were commissioned for syndication and O'Hanlon became Jetson again.

Among the more popular series in the staple situation comedy genre was "The Dick Van Dyke Show," one of television's classic comedies. With the title star playing Rob Petrie, a comedy writer for the fictional "The Alan Brady Show," the series started in 1961 and developed a large and loyal audience in its five years on the air.

Tiny Tim strumming a ukulele in an apperance with Dick Martin on "Laugh In" in 1968.

It spawned an even greater popularity for his co-star, Mary Tyler Moore, who began her own show in the 1970s.

"The Beverly Hillbillies" began in 1962 and became one of the longer-running situation comedies, with its last telecast in September 1971. The comedy centered on an Ozark hillbilly family who struck it rich with an oil well in their front yard. Buddy Ebsen and Irene Ryan co-starred. Reruns proved as popular as the originals.

"The Andy Griffith Show" placed among the top ten in ratings for its entire run from October 1960 to September 1968; two hundred and forty-nine episodes culminating in a No. 1 ranking in its final season. Andy Griffith played a sheriff in the fictional town of Mayberry, North Carolina, with Don Knotts as his deputy, Jim Nabors as gas station attendant Gomer Pyle, and Frances Bavier as Aunt Bee.

Nabors went on with his own show, "Gomer Pyle. U.S.M.C.," and "Andy Griffith" was succeeded by "Mayberry, R.F.D."

190

Mary Tyler Moore and Dick Van Dyke explaining the facts of life to their TV son Larry Matthews on the "Dick Van Dyke Show" in 1965.

Above: Buddy Ebsen in
costume for his starring role in
the "Beverly Hillbillies."

Below: Mary Tyler Moore,
starring in her own show.

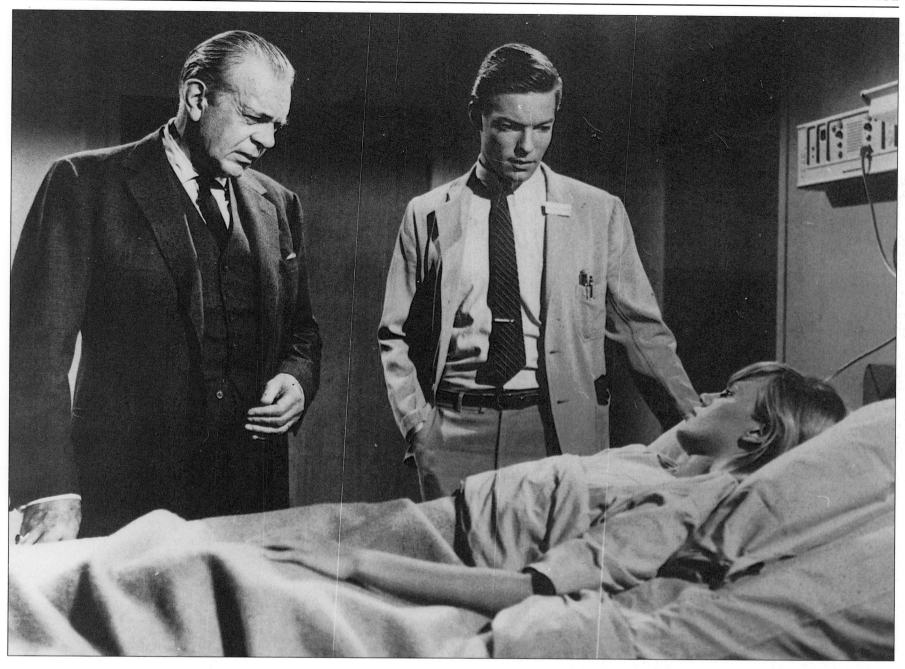

Facing page: the original cast of "Gilligan's Island" in 1964: (standing, left to right) Tina Louise, Jim Backus, Natalie Schafer, Alan Hale Jr., (seated, left to right) Bob Denver, Dawn Wells and Russell Johnson.

"Gilligan's Island," about a zany bunch of castaways on a deserted island, ran from 1964 to 1967 before going into syndication. The success of the shows' reruns led to a 1978 reunion of the cast members and two more sequel specials aired in 1979 and 1981.

"Monty Python's Flying Circus," the troupe that created the Ministry of Silly Walks and the fish-slapping dance, premiered on BBC on Sunday October 5, 1969 – in a slot previously filled by a religious discussion. The last original show was broadcast in December 1974.

The zany show was so popular in the United States that New York's Museum of Broadcasting marked the 20th anniversary of the program in 1989 with a ten-day retrospective.

If the doctor ordered a medical series then there were "Marcus Welby, M.D.," "Ben Casey," "Dr. Kildare," and "The Nurses."

Richard Chamberlain (on the right) in the title role of the series "Doctor Kildare," about a serious, hard-working young intern at Blair General Hospital. Raymond Massey (on the left) played the senior specialist Dr. Leonard Gillespie.

"Batman," a silly burlesque starring Adam West as the comic book hero, was a popular series. The villains were played by some of the finest fiends: Cesar Romero, Vincent Price, Burgess Meredith, and Maurice Evans among them.

Then there were the monster-family comedies like "The Addams Family" and "The Munsters."

Soaps remained standard fare and were joined by a rather curious newcomer. In the serial "Dark Shadows," Jonathan Frid played a vampire, Barnaby Collins, for an estimated six million viewers each afternoon, Monday-through-Friday. He noted once how soap plots were often devised according to the availability of the actors. When Frid needed several weeks off to make the film version of the story, imaginative writers chained him to a coffin for the duration of filming.

The Addams Family: (seated) Morticia (Carolyn Jones) with little Wednesday (Lisa Loring); (standing, left to right) Gomez, the head of the family (John Astin), Uncle Fester (Jackie Coogan), Lurch the butler (Ted Cassidy) and Granny (Blossom Rock).

194

Adam West as Batman, showing off his bat radio and batmobile in an episode of the 1966 series.

The "dynamic duo," Adam West and Burt Ward, in character as Batman and Robin (above) and in person (below).

196

Dan Rowan (left) and Dick Martin.

The comedy/variety genre was never the same after the debut of "Rowan and Martin's Laugh-In" in January 1968. (It was a one-time special on September 9, 1967.) Its fast-paced, seemingly haphazard style made it an instant success and created celebrities of its co-star hosts Dan Rowan and Dick Martin, as well as some of its regular performers. Judy Carne, Ruth Buzzi, Lily Tomlin, Jo Anne Worley and Goldie Hawn featured regularly, as did Gary Owens, Arte Johnson and Henry Gibson. The show's use of blackout sketches, one liners and cameo appearances by non-show business personalities was often imitated, but never topped. It was the No. 1 show in TV ratings for its first two full seasons, 1968-1970, and only ended its run in 1973. "Laugh In" catch phrases became part of the national language, from "Sock it to me!" to "You bet your bippy," and "Look that up in your *Funk and Wagnalls.*"

Sample closer:

Dick: "Can I tell you a story about my aunt?"

Dan: "I don't think we have time for that."

Dick: "My aunt was locked in a steambath for fourteen days with a live moose. I thought they might like to hear what she said when she came out."

Dan: "All right, what did she say?"

Dick: "My aunt said she was a lover of animals but never, ever trust a moose in a steambath for fourteen days. He may also be an Elk or a Shriner."

Dan: "Say good night, Dick."

Dick: "Good night, Dick."

197

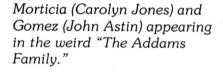

Morticia (Carolyn Jones) and Gomez (John Astin) appearing in the weird "The Addams Family."

198

Carol Burnett in character on the "Carol Burnett Show."

"The Smothers Brothers Comedy Hour" was another popular comedy-variety show of the '60s. The comic singing team of Tom and Dick Smothers were an irreverent pair and their show topical and funny, appealing primarily to younger viewers.

At times, their irreverence got them into trouble with CBS censors. NBC had similar problems with "Saturday Night Live." Some advertisers backed out of both programs. The Smothers brothers' show often featured anti-Vietnam guests like Pete Seeger, and poked fun at everything from motherhood to religion. CBS dropped the show abruptly in May 1973, replacing it, temporarily at first, with the syndicated "Hee Haw," a kind of country music "Laugh-In" with cornball humor that became a big hit itself.

Comedy-variety shows appeared to be losing their audiences – that is except for Carol Burnett's shows. After establishing

"Saturday Night Live" madness with the "Loopners." Enid (Jane Curtin) is offering sustenance to Todd (Bill Murray) and her daughter Lisa (Gilda Radner).

200

Garry Moore on his boat Little Toot *with Durward Kirby.*

herself on "The Garry Moore Show" between 1959 and 1962, she began her own "The Carol Burnett Show" in 1967. With its regular troupe, including Harvey Korman, Tim Conway and Vicki Lawrence in a vaudevillian format of comic sketches, it remained popular and successful throughout 1978. Burnett's talents as a comedienne, singer, dancer and actress carried it through.

The adventure/intrigue series "Mission Impossible" began every episode the same way: the leader of a group of special government agents would be given an assignment. This arrived via a tape recording that began: "Your mission, should you choose to accept it … " It concluded: "This tape will self-destruct in five seconds."

The 1966-1973 series starred Peter Graves (a hero despite his never-to-be-forgotten movie role as the German spy in "Stalag 17"), Barbara Bain, Martin Landau, Greg Morris and Peter Lupus. It was remade in the '80s, prompted by a writers' strike.

Left: "Mod Squad" members (from left to right) Michael Cole, Peggy Lipton and Clarence Williams III.

Below: on the series "My Favorite Martian," martian Uncle Martin (Ray Walson) conversed with animals such as George the dog. Tim O'Hara (played by Bill Bixby) looks on unimpressed.

Below: Marta Kristen, Mark Goddard, June Lockhart and Guy Williams, dressed for action on "Lost in Space."

"Get Smart" was a spoof of spy films starring Don Adams as the not-so-smart secret agent Maxwell Smart. Smart worked with beautiful Agent 99 (originally Barbara Feldon) to defeat the bad guys of K.A.O.S., who planned to take over the world, "Would you believe?"

Detective stories were always popular fodder for television, and "Peter Gunn" (1958-1961) was one of the best. It starred Craig Stevens and Lola Albright with Herschel Berndardi as Lieutenant Jacoby in a sophisticated private eye series greatly enhanced by Henry Mancini's original jazz themes.

September 6, 1966, is something of an international holiday to a cult known as "Trekkies." It is the date of the first telecast of the futuristic series, "Star Trek," which covered the adventures of the starship *Enterprise* in the twenty-third century.

Captain James Kirk (William Shatner), the alien first officer Dr. Spock (Leonard Nimoy), Dr. "Bones" McCoy (DeForest Kelley) and chief engineer Montgomery "Scotty" Scott (James Doohan) became idols to the program's watchers.

202

Sally Field in the 1967 comedy series "The Flying Nun," in which, with the aid of a strong wind and an unusual cornet, she occasionally took flight.

Facing page: Don Adams as special agent Maxwell Smart, complete with shoe telephone in the spy spoof series "Get Smart."

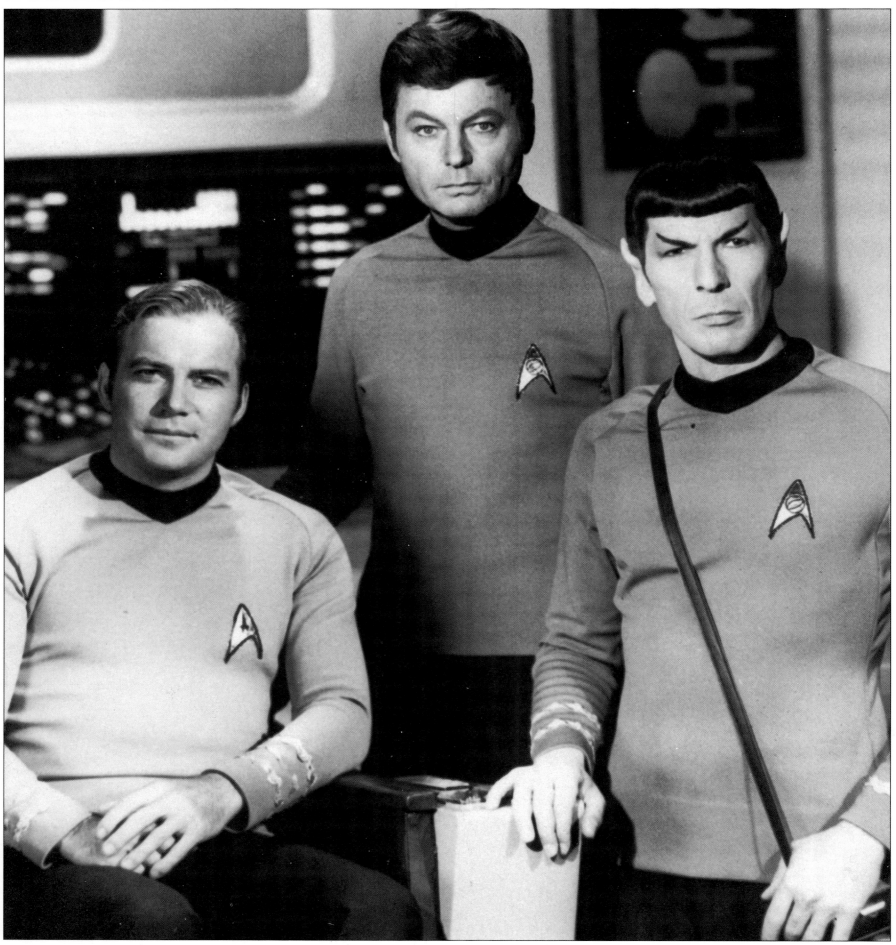

Oddly, the series was not very popular at the start, though it became a sensation after it had been on the air for quite some time. (It placed fifty-second among all series in its first season.) But its success in reruns and syndication has been nothing short of phenomenal, spewing off a whole industry of "Star Trek"-related merchandise. "Star Trek: The Next Generation," became the most successful hour-long drama in syndication. There have been five motion pictures and more than sixty "Star Trek" novels – selling some eighteen million copies. There have also been books about the making of the series and the movies, including "Captain's Log: William Shatner's Personal Account of the Making of Star Trek V: The Final Frontier," as told to his daughter. Then, for trekkie junkies, there's "The Star Trek Compendium."

There was now much to fill this "wasteland," some of it meaty and significant, much of it inane and soporific – "junk food for the eyes" was one description.

But, there was no disputing that television had firmly established itself in our lives. It was part of the family, part of society, part of our political structure, part of the American psyche.

It was about to show it could be out of this world.

Facing page: the trio that made "Star Trek" one of TV's most popular adventures: (from left to right) William Shatner as Captain Kirk, De Forest Kelley as Dr. "Bones" McCoy, and Leonard Nimoy as the alien first officer, Mr. Spock, a half-bred Vulcan with pointy ears.

205

Below: food throwing was one of the milder exploits in "Soap," described as an "adult character comedy series." Characters Chester Tate (on the left) and Burt Campbell were played by Robert Mandan and Richard Mulligan respectively.

Chapter V

The Great Obsession

It was the greatest show off earth.

After the twentieth day of July, in the year 1969 by earthly Christian reckoning, the moon was no longer a mystery, no longer a visionary virgin for poets, peasants, romanticists and writers. Man stepped on its surface.

In the person of Neil Alden Armstrong, man landed and walked on the moon, followed by a second man, Edwin E. Aldrin Jr. It seemed an inconceivable occurrence.

Television showed us it wasn't. Television, in effect, monitored civilization in evolution. It was a momentous occasion, one for which parents kept the children up late to watch — or woke them so as not to miss it.

Explaining how TV covered such an event is much like trying to explain how the moon mission itself was conceived and executed. Explaining how the television signal came from the surface of the moon to the NASA ground station in Parke, Australia, some two hundred and forty thousand miles away, is hard enough. To cover its journey onwards, via Pacific satellite to the U.S. ground station at Jamesburg, California, then by land line to Mission Control in Houston, Texas, and to the pool network link, is mind-blowing!

The main problems in covering the event were: i, making enough time to get all the preparation done; ii, creating a sense of perspective for a historic event of this import (and uncertainty); iii, the thirty continuous hours of coverage and iv, making the very special story informative and at the same time entertaining.

Network producers described it as "inventiveness and creativity of coverage" and "creativity in concert with a lot of homework."

Each of the networks set up special "Space Center" studios and control rooms in New York. These were filled with full-size or scale models of command module, lunar landing module, earth globes, moonscapes, maps — in short, everything necessary to recreate the complete mission.

It all worked out to perfection, as did the real moon landing — these were television's finest hours.

It cost an estimated $13 million, but it was, as CBS executive producer Robert Wussler said, "the world's greatest single broadcast."

Another major current event provided television with even

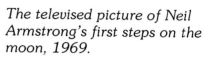

The televised picture of Neil Armstrong's first steps on the moon, 1969.

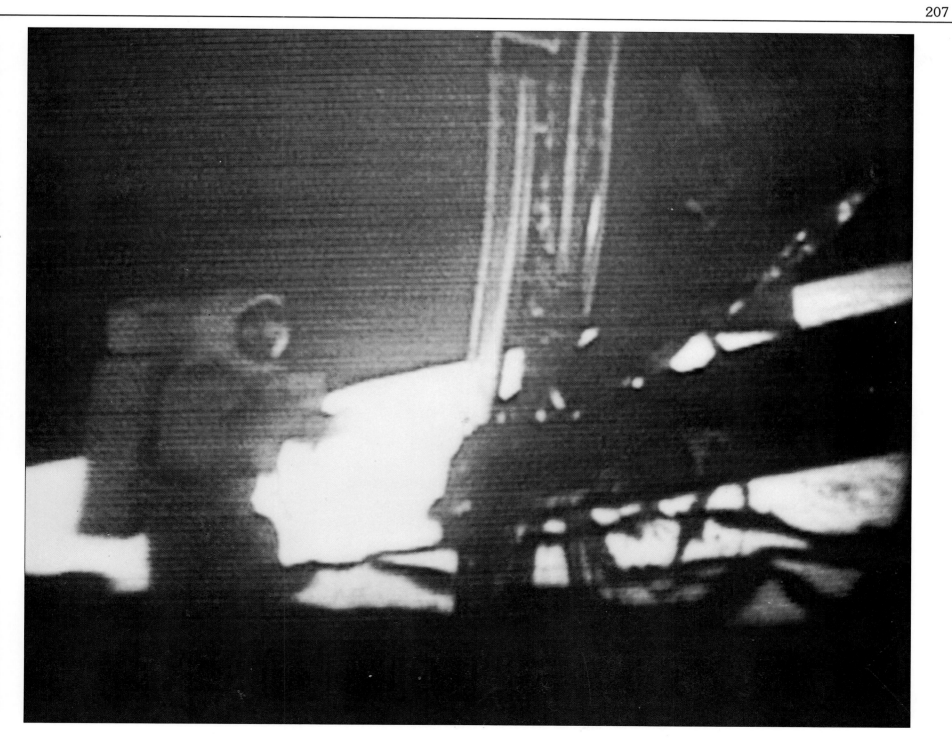

more coverage credit – but not at first. When news of a break-in at Democratic Party offices was first revealed, no one thought much of it, including television. The Washington Post investigated deeper, however, until the Watergate scandal reached the top of the White House.

When further evidence accumulated Congress decided to hold hearings on the matter, and public television leapt for the opportunity to present the hearings live. The Corporation for Public Broadcasting had been established in 1967, but had to rely on Congressional funding on a year-to-year basis. In 1972, it had been authorized $155 million for two years. It wasn't much, but the Watergate hearings helped it gain new support. With the hearings, live by day and repeated on tape at night, public broadcasting stations got the highest ratings in their existence.

Commercial television also decided to carry the hearings, rotating the coverage among themselves.

The Watergate scandal proved a hit with audiences; in one week in July 1973, it was first (NBC), third (ABC) and eighth (CBS) in audience ratings (which did not include noncommercial television).

Senator Sam Ervin, as committe chairman, became a popular figure in his folksy way, as viewers watched hour upon hour of testimony. The charges against the Nixon administration involved spying, bribery, burglary and perjury. Television continued its coverage through the beginning of the impeachment process.

On August 8, 1974, President Richard Nixon appeared on television to announce his resignation from office.

The "greatest show off earth," television coverage of the first steps on the moon.

Walter Cronkite on CBS during the flight of Apollo 11.

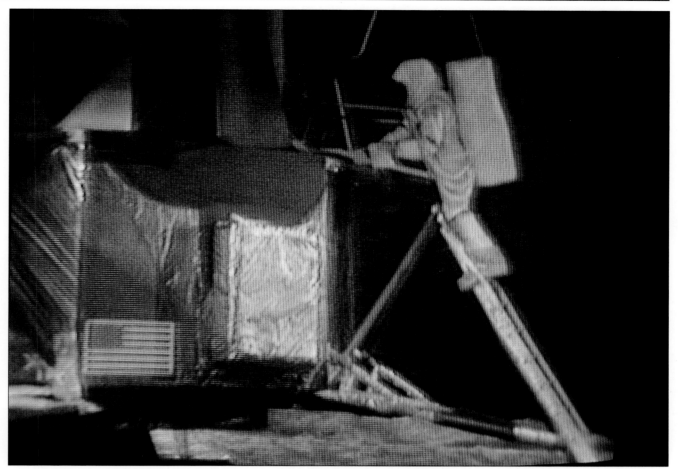

Television had played a role in the historic fall of a president, and provided the medium by which he had called an end to it.

Watergate was unique, but investigative television was a regular feature of "60 Minutes," a provocative show covering politics on an international scale as well as domestic debate. The program, which began in 1968, was originally hosted by newsmen Mike Wallace and Harry Reasoner, later with Morley Safer, then Dan Rather, Ed Bradley and Diane Sawyer.

But TV still had to deal with the more mundane as well. The staples consisted of Saturday morning cartoons, late weeknight talk shows, documentaries and dramas, situation comedies and quiz shows, daytime soap operas and nighttime movies. And sports.

President Richard Nixon announcing his resignation from office on television in 1974.

210

Bob Hope and Jimmy Durante on a comedy special in 1967.

Whatever we were watching in the 1970s, we were watching more of it. There were now more color television sets than black-and-white. There were two, or even three, TV sets in each household. Typically there would be one for the family in the living room, one in the kids' room and, perhaps, one in the kitchen – where bacon and eggs were joined by the early morning news and weather. Or there might be a set in the bedroom, where Johnny Carson was likely to be the last face seen before lights out. We spent more time with television now that there was something to see from dawn to near-dawn. There were by now an estimated three thousand hours of programming in prime-time, from more than seven hundred TV stations – numbers that were to continue to grow.

The numbers were certainly not lost on the salesmen, the sponsors of television shows. Commercial television's role, in a sense, is to deliver audiences to sponsors. The matter of ratings and demographics (how many are watching and who is watching what) is therefore of great import. The commercials themselves don't sell products, they sell hopes and dreams – of love, sex, fame, and power. Wear these clothes, they say, and it's straight to the executive suite. Drink this beer, they say, and you'll attract the opposite sex. Advertising had always played a role in television, though some had hoped it wouldn't. When Herbert Hoover was U.S. Secretary of Commerce in the 1920s, he had urged broadcasters to keep advertising out of it. Broadcasting would be destroyed, he said, if ever a presidential message were to become "the meat in a sandwich of two patent medicine advertisements."

There have been numerous efforts to restrict advertising on television ever since, as critics complain that the medium is not only the message, but the marketplace; that TV has become a

212

A sales pitch is a sales pitch is a …

Sale ends Sat. Night

shopping center. But it cannot be forgotten, or ignored, that television under a free enterprise arrangement is a profit-making venture and that most of that money is supplied by advertising.

Advertising was nothing new – radio had had commercial jingles. The early days of television made the sponsors obvious, though. Titles included "The Texaco Star Theater" (the Milton Berle show), "The Bell Telephone Hour," and "Kraft Television Theater." Remember "Speedy" Alka Seltzer? And who can forget the Old Gold Dancing Packs – leggy dancers inside a cigarette-pack-costume tap dancing their message to the tune of "Sidewalks of New York" back in 1948. (Cigarette commercials were banned from television in 1971.)

In the early years, the sponsors and their advertising agencies

Johnny Carson with guest Liberace on his late-night show in 1984.

213

214

were chiefly, if not directly, responsible for the programming.

On an early "Playhouse 90" presentation of "Judgment at Nuremberg" (a powerful story of Nazi inhumanity) there was no mention made of gas ovens. It was, however, sponsored by a gas association. There were numerous other examples of sponsor interference, especially from cigarette manufacturers who insisted their product be shown only in the best light.

But by the end of the 1950s the networks had taken control of their product.

Sponsors still remain vulnerable to viewer complaints, however.

In more recent times some sponsors have been forced to withdraw their commercials from what was felt to be an offending program. A couple of sponsors pulled their commercials from the

Facing page: Dick Cavett getting a lift from guests Muhammad Ali and Joe Frazier on his show in 1974.

The Philco "Predicta" television receiver, introduced in 1958, was the first in which the tube was separate from the chassis. The "separate screen" received the picture signals from the chassis (on the right) through a twenty-five-foot cord.

215

Alien "Alf," on his own show.

The Smothers Brothers, Tom (below) and Dick.

prime-time "Married ... With Children," for example, after a mother campaigned against what she considered to be its "off-color" humor.

There were complaints, too, about the number of commercials, their placement and their repetition. The networks stretched thirty-second commercial breaks to forty seconds, providing four ten-second commercials between programs – and more advertising revenue. The National Association of Broadcasters tried setting some industry guidelines for commercials, including the amount of time that they could occupy, but they seemed to be widely ignored.

By the 1970s, the TV commercial, that stodgy gray necessary evil in the entertainment medium, had come into its own. Its music, humor and technique often reflected more imagination and artistry than the show it interrupted.

Commercials had gained at least a grudging acceptance, if not some respect, from audiences and actors alike. No longer did

stage and screen actors reject advertising work as demeaning to their talents. Veteran stars did commercials, for substantial pay, and budding starlets hoping for future roles in television or the movies used the exposure they offered.

Commercial making became a competitive business in itself; resulting in soaring production costs. One ad agency wag wrote about it in a book called "Down the Tube, or Making Television Commercials is Such a Dog-Eat-Dog Business, No Wonder They're Called Spots." Commercial makers even started their own recognition awards, the "Clios," for categories from automobiles to pharmaceuticals.

Sexual innuendo began to play a role in commercials; its ageless appeal was utilized to sell everything from cars to cereal. Swedish beauty Gunilla Knutson helped her acting career by purring "Take it t'off, take it t'all off" for a TV commercial for shaving cream. Barbara Feldon wound up co-starring in "Get Smart" after hawking a line of men's toiletries while stretched out

Pee Wee Herman on "Pee Wee's Playhouse."

218

Clara Peller in the Wendy's commercial "Where's the beef?"

on a tigerskin rug. Similarly, Pamela Austin earned roles in movies and television after a career selling cars on TV. Even animated salesmen became stars: Charlie the Tuna, the Jolly Green Giant and Mr. Clean.

Some of the more popular ones of recent years include:

– "Where's the Beef," a Wendy's commercial that made a star of the late Clara Peller.

– "I ate the whole thing," for Alka-Seltzer.

– Any "Pepsi Generation" spot.

– California raisins (which later begat its own children's cartoon show).

– Nike sneakers commercials with superstar athletes Michael Jordan and Bo "Bo Knows" Jackson.

– Bud Light beer spokesdog "Spuds MacKenzie."

Nowadays, television commercials are often a showcase for visual experimentation; quick cuts, flashy graphics, unusual special effects and daring cinematography are no longer the exception, but the rule. The commercial market has become lucrative enough for a number of major studios and production companies to launch their own commercial units. The price for a thirty-second commercial during the 1990 Super Bowl was $700,000. George Lucas of "Star Wars" fame even established Lucasfilm Commercial Productions.

Once looked down upon by Hollywood directors, commercial film-making is now appealing to the best of them – to the score of $20,000 a day. With some spots costing $1 million, a

219

Spuds MacKenzie, star of Budweiser Light beer commercials, with friends.

commercial director can spend significantly more money per minute on an ad than on a movie.

The better ads are perhaps those that tell a story quickly and convincingly – they can grab the attention of a generation bombarded by all sorts of sights and sounds and hold it for ten or thirty seconds. TV ads are compressed, giving more information in a shorter time span – more "bang for the buck." But does it eliminate the process of experiencing, savoring, or even thinking?

Much like the programs they sponsor, TV ads change with fickle public tastes. Music was a big part of successful commercials for a while, then it was humor, then razzle and dazzle *with* music and humor. Admired celebrities were popular in the sale of soft drinks in the 1980s.

Advertising agencies saw a trend toward animated and fantasy spots in the late 1980s.

A survey of the most popular commercials of 1989 had McDonald's at the top, followed by Pepsi and Diet Pepsi,

220

The cast of the popular family sitcom "Family Ties."

California Raisins, Energizer batteries and Isuzu vehicles. Rounding out the top ten were Bud Light, Coca-Cola, Miller Lite, Infiniti and Nike.

While commercials are an accepted fact of life in any "free," non-government-run television system, many people refuse to accept their contents. This is especially true when they are aimed at children, considered to be a particularly vulnerable audience.

It is estimated that sponsors spend $500 million a year promoting all kinds of goodies to young consumers through television.

Consumer advocacy groups have often petitioned government agencies for some control over the quantity and type of commercials on kids' shows. Some of their studies have shown that children are exposed to far more toy, cereal and candy advertising per hour than adults. One legislator called it "crass commercialization" of children's television, where the constant din of cereal, toy and candy ads "is enough to make any child's – and any parent's – head pound and stomach ache."

TV sets seem to spring up everywhere, even in airport lounges.

222

Sally Jessy Raphael, hostess of her own syndicated talk show, surrounded by children at a taping in the St. Louis studios.

The cast of "Good Times" (left to right): Bernadene Satanis as Thelma, Esther Rolle as Florida and John Amos as James.

Some of the advertising to children is considered to be deceptive. "Too often we do our worst advertising and direct it at kids" claimed Peggy Charren, founder of the group "Action for Children's Television" (ACT). The group was established in 1968 to encourage informative children's television. ACT would impose on broadcasters the "three R's" of television: restriction, requirement and reporting.

A half-hour program produced by the Consumers Union, "Buy Me That!," described as "a kids' survival guide to TV advertising," tried to explain to youngsters that on television, "what you see isn't always what you get." At one time there was a restriction on the number of ads on children's shows – no more than nine-and-a-half minutes per hour. However, this restriction was repealed by the FCC in 1984. Since then, some have measured as many as fourteen minutes of commercials per hour on weekdays and eleven minutes per hour on weekends.

Children's programming itself took a giant leap forward in the '70s, with the introduction of "Sesame Street."

Developed by Jane Ganz Cooney of the Children's Television Workshop, "Sesame Street" had financial support from the U.S. Office of Education, the Ford Foundation and the Carnegie Corporation. The fast-paced program was aimed at pre-schoolers and used songs, puppets and animation in a city-street-setting to teach letters, numbers and simple sentences.

Today, English-language versions of "Sesame Street" are seen in more than eighty countries and the show has fifteen international co-productions. It now costs about $12 million a year to make (eighty percent of which comes from commercial licensing of its

223

Jack Lord relaxing with actress Nancy Kwan during a break in the filming of "Hawaii Five–0" in 1968.

characters, the remainder from Public Broadcasting Stations) but Jane Ganz Cooney remembers the beginnings:

"I said, 'Let's do a kind of "Laugh-In" for kids … and let's not have a single host. Let's have at least four hosts who will be men, women, black, white, Hispanic and so on." She also wanted each show interrupted by "non-commercials" to teach letters and numbers.

Appearing in the first "Sesame Street" shows in 1969 were the "Muppets," the puppet creations of Jim Henson – a critical decision in the show's success. Children watching were enthralled by the likes of Kermit the Frog, Oscar the Grouch, Ernie, Bert, the Cookie Monster and Big Bird (a giant yellow bird costume originally worn by Frank Oz).

U.S. network officials didn't think adults would accept the Muppets, so "The Muppet Show" was syndicated and produced in England before it was shown in the United States. It was shown in America from 1976 to 1981 and became the most popular

The influential and highly praised "Sesame Street."

224

Above: stars of the "A Team,"
1985.

Below: Jim Henson, creator of
the Muppets, with Kermit the
Frog.

226

Right: Kermit the Frog in his role as editor of The Muppet Show News.

Fleet (on the right) gets the lowdown on the news with Miss Piggy and Link Snout, captain of the starship Swinetrek, in a 1977 episode of "The Muppet Show." The series was recorded at England's Borehamwood studios.

first-run syndicated series in TV, reaching hundreds of millions of viewers in more than one hundred countries. The Muppets became an inudstry of their own, with more than four hundred characters merchandised, the "Muppet Movie" – and a "Miss Piggy" calendar.

Other Children's Television Worskshop programs followed, including "The Electric Company" in 1971. Aimed primarily at seven to ten year olds, this show stressed reading skills and regularly faetured Bill Cosby and Rita Moreno. In later years, the science show, "3-2-1 Contact" and the math show, "Square One TV," joined children's TV.

One of the more beloved of children's television heroes was Mister Rogers, whose "Mister Rogers Neighborhood" began in 1962, produced by WQED in Pittsburg, Pa. It became the longest running show on public television. Fred Mcfeely Rogers attracted more than ten million young viewers a week with his gentle demeanor.

The cast of "The Electric Company" in 1971: (left to right) Judy Graubart as TV chef Julia Grownup, Morgan Freeman as Easy Reader, Lee Chamberlain as a fortune teller, Rita Moreno as a vaudeville clown, Bill Cosby in costume as a musketeer and Skip Hinnant as word detective Fargo North, Decoder.

227

228

Lucille Ball, perhaps the most popular TV star of all time.

Even so, quality children's shows were still few and far between.

Peggy Charren, ACT president, once suggested that producers and presenters of children's programming ask themselves some questions to determine the quality of their show:

– Does the program have something to say instead of just something to sell?

– Would you submit it to an international animation or film festival for an award?

– Would you put it at the top of the list for the lawyer who is defending you against a station's challenge?

– Would parents tape it if their children were at the dentist?

– Would you mention it by name if your child's teacher asked you what you did for a living?

While children's programming continued to be a subject of concern, if not dispute, TV for adults was beginning to tackle subjects neither sponsors nor networks would previously have touched in "family time."

Mr. Television, Milton Berle.

TV personality Steve Allen in 1959.

"All in the Family" was a leading example. Developed by producer Norman Lear – from the British series, "Til Death Do Us Part" – it revolved around an amiable, uneducated white bigot in a working class neighborhood who was blatantly outspoken in his prejudices. It was a comedy.

Carroll O'Connor played the lead role of Archie Bunker, with Jean Stapleton as Edith "Dingbat" Bunker, Sally Struthers as daughter Gloria and Rob Reiner as son-in-law Mike Stivic ("Meathead").

Its harsh realities shook up the TV world, but huge audiences, once accustomed to its outrageous humor, made it one of the most successful of TV's regulars. It was first telecast on September 21, 1971, and held the No. 1 ratings position for five straight years. The last of the original shows was seen in 1983.

The show has been re-run often and copied in numerous places, including South Africa where it emerged as "People Like Us." It also engendered several new spinoff series including "The

230

"All in the Family," 1975.

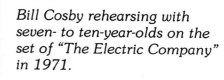

*Bill Cosby rehearsing with
seven- to ten-year-olds on the
set of "The Electric Company"
in 1971.*

*"Mister Rogers," at rehearsals
with some of his puppet
friends in Pittsburgh.*

232

Anchorman Dan Rather at his CBS desk.

Jeffersons" (the black family neighbors), "Maude" (Edith Bunker's cousin on "All in the Family") and "Good Times" (based on Maude's maid).

"The Mary Tyler Moore Show" debuted in 1970 and lasted seven highly successful seasons, breaking new ground within traditional network television foundations. It dealt with a single career woman, and dealt with her realistically, though not without humor. Mary Tyler Moore, as Mary Richards, symbolized the independent woman of the '70s, a broadcast journalist with professional, but little romantic, success.

(In a different form, the subject was to return in "Murphy Brown" in the '80s.)

"The Mary Tyler Moore Show" spun off "Lou Grant," a newspaper drama with Ed Asner, and "Phyllis," with the landlady, Cloris Leachman. "The Mary Tyler Moore Show" also featured a popular character named Rhoda Morgenstern. Presto: the "Rhoda" series, with Valerie Harper, in 1974. Another well-

The 200th show of "The Jeffersons," celebrated by (left to right) Marla Gibbs, Sherman Hemsley, Isabel Sanford, producer Norman Lear, Ned Wertimer, Berlinda Tolbert, Roxie Roker and Franklin Cover.

received comedy series, "The Odd Couple," was based on Neil Simon's play and movie of the same name. The TV series starred Jack Klugman as the gruff, sloppy sportswriter Oscar Madison and Tony Randall as his fastidious roommate, the photographer Felix Unger.

Television continued to introduce new family situation comedies, the bread-and-butter shows of prime-time.

"The Brady Bunch" was one that endured. It was an old-fashioned, sweet and harmless half-hour show about a middle-class family with six children – a widow with three daughters and a widower with three sons.

(Can you name the six children?)

(Marcia, Greg, Jan, Peter, Cindy and Bobby.)

The show, with Robert Reed and Florence Henderson as the parents, ran from September 1969 through August 1974, with reruns appearing in daytime hours the next year. There was a comedy-variety series in 1977, "The Brady Bunch Hour," but it

The cast of "The Mary Tyler Moore Show," which ended its long run in 1977: (top row, left to right) Ted Knight, Gavin MacLeod, Edward Asner, (seated, left to right) Betty White, Georgia Engel and Mary Tyler Moore.

234

Facing page: "The Brady Bunch" in 1975.

236

The Beatles on "The Ed Sullivan Show" in 1964.

Gilda Radner as Roseanne Rosannadanna on "Saturday Night Live," failing to impress Jane Curtin.

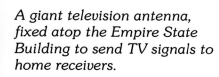

A giant television antenna, fixed atop the Empire State Building to send TV signals to home receivers.

238

Facing page: Fonzie, played by Henry Winkler, is harassed by some toughs (Garry Springer and Larry Golden) in the "A Mind of Their Own" episode of "Happy Days."

Nostalgic, light-hearted "Happy Days" starred Ron Howard (center) as Richie Cunningham and Anson Williams (right) as Potsie, and featured pony-tailed bobbysoxers such as Kathy O'Dare (left).

only lasted five months. In 1981, the "Bunch" returned in a spinoff situation comedy, "The Brady Brides," and was again "reborn" as "The Bradys."

A similarly wholesome family series was "The Partridge Family." It ran from 1970 to 1974 and starred Shirley Jones as the head of a family that becomes a rock 'n' roll band. The show also featured Susan Dey and David Cassidy.

A situation comedy of a different sort, "Happy Days" took a nostalgic trip back to the 1950s. It premiered in 1974, the story of two high school kids – Richie Cunningham (played by Ron Howard) and "Potsie" Weber (Anson Williams) – and their buddies. The guys hung out at a malt shop called Arnold's Drive-In. With the later introduction of the cool character of Arthur "Fonzie" Fonzarelli (Henry Winkler), the show took on new aspects – and new success, lasting until 1984.

The leather jacket that "the Fonz" wore on "Happy Days" is enshrined in the national museum, the Smithsonian Institution (along with Archie Bunker's chair from "All in the Family" and other television memorabilia).

Two characters who appeared briefly on "Happy Days," Laverne De Fazio (Penny Marshall) and Shirley Feeney (Cindy Williams), went on to star in their own separate show. The comedy series "Laverne and Shirley" was also set in Milwaukee in the 1950s, like "Happy Days." This hit story of two girls working in a brewery had a No. 1 ranking in the 1977-78 season.

239

240

Professional golfer Curtis Strange waving to the crowd after his victory at the 1989 U.S. Open.

Sports events had been stalwarts of television programming since the earliest days. Their fast-paced, unpredictable action seemed "made" for the visual medium and vicarious armchair athletes, whether the sport was boxing, baseball, tennis or track.

In 1961, ABC begun something different in sports, "Wide World of Sports," a two-hour magazine-style format combining live, taped and filmed events from around the world. It gained large weekend audiences and has done so ever since.

In the mid '60s, Saturday afternoons in the fall were college football days, and Sunday afternoons became professional football afternoons, much to the profit of the networks and their affiliates.

Then, on a Monday night in September 1970, ABC began its run of regularly scheduled programmes under the title "Monday Night Football," opening the floodgates to a rush of sports that continues unstemmed. A three-man announcing crew for the National Football League Games consisted of the caustic Howard Cosell, play-by-play broadcaster Keith Jackson and former football star Don Meredith. (Frank Gifford took over from Jackson the second season.)

The success was immediate and astounding. In an effort to regain lost patronage because of the game on TV, some movie theaters promoted their own "NFL" (Night for Ladies) to lure the football "widows" out to the big screen. "Monday Night Football" celebrated its twentieth anniversary in the 1989-90 season. Much of its success was due to technology; "instant replay," developed in the mid-1960s, had became a standard sports technique and

241

During NBC's broadcast of the Super Bowl in 1989, Tim Krumrie (seen here diving over the ten-yard line), of the Cincinnati Bengals, broke a leg.

did much to explain the intricacies of the game to an ever-widening audience.

Its success released funding for other sports – players and team owners alike – as well as profitting television; networks and independent locals competed fiercely for contracts. College football contracts with television in the five years beginning 1991 brought the College Football Association $300 million. In 1989, the New York Yankees baseball team signed a ten-year local TV contract for $500 million – despite Marshall McLuhan's claim that baseball was too static and too individual a sport for the TV Age. TV still fulfilled the desires of those who weren't satisfied by sport alone, however.

A significant audience was mesmerized in 1976 by the twelve-hour dramatic miniseries, "Rich Man, Poor Man," from Irwin Shaw's novel about the divergent lives of two brothers after World War II. It was so successful that it was repeated the following year and spawned a sequel, "Rich Man, Poor Man – Book II."

The success of "Rich Man, Poor Man" was quickly overshadowed by "Roots," the most-watched dramatic show in television history. (In actual fact it was an extended special). An estimated one hundred million viewers saw the final of eight installments in January 1977 – nearly half the country's population.

"Roots" was based on Alex Haley's novel of his own African roots, beginning in West Africa in 1750 and continuing right up to the American Civil War. The program was repeated the following year, again over a one-week period, and a sequel,

242

Joy entered the slave quarters when Bell (Madge Sinclair) married Kunta Kinte (John Amos) in "Roots."

Ben Vereen as Chicken George, the fighting-cock trainer in "Roots."

244

TV talk show host Phil Donahue in ladies clothes on his show about cross-dressing, which featured a transvestite fashion show and cross-dressing guest, Melody.

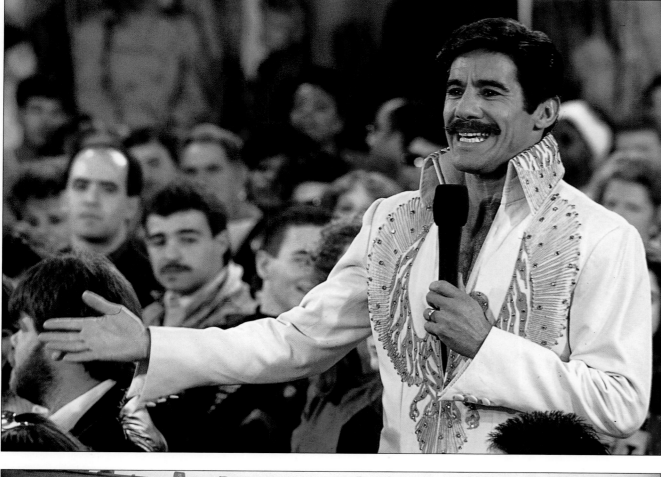

Geraldo Rivera in an Elvis Presley-style jumpsuit on an episode of his show, "Geraldo," celebrating the rock and roll legend.

"The Day After," a popular but controversial TV movie about the aftermath of a nuclear explosion, broadcast in 1983.

"Roots: The Next Generation," appeared two years after that. Perhaps the most popular serial of the '70s, and then some, was "M*A*S*H." Superb scripts, fine acting, humor and realistic drama were combined in this series about the 4077th Mobile Army Surgical Hospital during the Korean war.

Based on Robert Altman's 1970 film starring Elliot Gould and Donald Sutherland (in turn based on Richard Hooker's novel of the same name), M*A*S*H started its lengthy and successful run in 1972. It was a favorite for two hundred and fifty-one episodes in eleven seasons. It lasted far longer than the war itself. Characters such as Captain Benjamin Franklin "Hawkeye" Pierce (Alan Alda), Captain John "Trapper" McIntire (Wayne Rogers), Lieutenant Colonel Henry Blake (McLean Stevenson), Major Margaret "Hot Lips" Houlihan (Loretta Swit) and Major Frank Burns (Larry Linville) became household names. Corporal Walter "Radar" O'Reilly (Gary Burghoff), Father John Mulcahy (William Christopher) and Corporal Max Klinger (Jamie Farr) also became

*Below left: the original cast of "M*A*S*H," (left to right) Larry Linville, Loretta Swit, Wayne Rogers, Gary Burghoff, McLean Stevenson and (seated) Alan Alda. Below right: the cast of the final episode in 1983 (top, left to right) William Christopher, Jamie Farr, (standing, left to right) Mike Farrell, Harry Morgan, Loretta Swit, David Ogden and (seated) Alan Alda.*

246

a regular part of the family on Saturday nights. The team's exploits, romances, practical jokes and serious fears were followed with regularity and devotion.

When its last episode, the two-and-a-half hour special "Goodbye, Farewell and Amen," was aired on February 28, 1983, it was the most widely-seen television program of all time – topping the "who shot J.R.?" episode of "Dallas" in 1980!

Now, considering the obsessional following that that 1978 soap opera received, that was some accomplishment.

The granddaddy of the prime-time soap opera was "Peyton Place." Broadcast twice – and sometimes three times – a week, the serial ran between 1964 and 1969. The continuing tale of the gossipy goings-on in a small New England town was followed by "Harold Robbins' The Survivors," which appeared only briefly in 1969. Other failed efforts at the genre included "Sons and Daughters," "Beacon Hill," "Executive Suite" and "W.E.B."

Then there was "Dallas."

247

*"M*A*S*H" in 1982.*

Introduced on April 2, 1978, "Dallas" was the story of two generations of the oil-rich Ewing family of Texas and their adversaries, the Barnes family. As the plots and schemes thickened the show's popularity soared and J.R. Ewing (Larry Hagman) became one of television's most dastardly villains. (His cowboy hat is on display at the Smithsonian.)

At the end of the 1979-80 season, somebody shot J.R. Viewers wouldn't find out whodunnit until the next season. The suspense caused a great deal of speculation in the press and an avalanche of mail pointing the finger at one "Dallas" character or another. It inspired "Who Shot J.R?" contests on both sides of the Atlantic, as well as songs, T-shirts and "Dallas" merchandise. To ensure secrecy, five different endings were filmed and scripts kept under lock and key. Finally, fans learned that J.R. was not dead but merely wounded. The November 21, 1980 episode, on which it was revealed who had pulled the trigger, was the most widely watched single show up to that time. (It was Kristin, Sue Ellen's younger sister, who had fired the gun.)

"Dallas" rivals among prime-time soaps included "Dynasty," which lasted nine years, "Knots Landing" and "Falcon Crest."

248

The cast of "Dallas."

The wedding of "Dynasty" characters Adam Carrington (Gordon Thompson) and Dana Waring (Leann Hunley) took place in 1987. Guests included (on the left) Mr and Mrs Blake Carrington (John Forsyth and Linda Evans) and Alexis Carrington (Joan Collins) was bridesmaid.

Blake and Alexis get to grips in "Dynasty."

250

The cast of the serial "Falcon Crest," which premiered in 1981 with Jane Wyman (center) as wealthy Californian vintner Angie Channing.

Public television had its highlights, too – mostly imported from Britain.

"Masterpiece Theater," an anthology series of drama, began in January 1971. It was funded by a grant from Mobil Oil and was hosted by Alistair Cooke. Public TV's most successful and popular series, however, running between 1974 and 1977, was London Weekend Television's "Upstairs, Downstairs." The fifty-five-episode-long series concerned members of a wealthy London family and their several servants. It spanned the first three decades of the 20th century. (Some earlier episodes were never shown in the United States.)

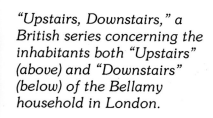

"Upstairs, Downstairs," a British series concerning the inhabitants both "Upstairs" (above) and "Downstairs" (below) of the Bellamy household in London.

Another bright light of the '70s was "Saturday Night Live." This comedy-variety show was first telecast on network television in 1975. It was to have a great influence on similar programs in the future, and on the lives and careers of many of its performers.

A late-night show, "Saturday Night Live" featured "The Not Ready for Prime-Time Players" among numerous new – and often outrageous – comedy talents. These included Chevy Chase, who opened the "Weekend Update" skit with "Good evening, I'm Chevy Chase, and you're not" and then did one of his pratfalls. John Belushi, Dan Akroyd, Gilda Radner, Garrett Morris, Jane Curtin, Laraine Newman, Bill Murray, Joe Piscopo, Eddie Murphy, Billy Crystal, and announcer Don Pardo also starred. The show made much of guest hosts, from George Carlin (host of the first telecast), to Candice Bergen (later "Murphy Brown"), Elliott Gould, Dick Cavett – and "Anyone Can Host" contest winner Mrs. Miskel Spillman. Jim Henson's "Muppets" were a regular feature.

The host Dick Cavett transferred from a talk-variety show (1969-1972) to a straight variety show (1973-1975) to a late-night talk-discussion show (1986). The latter was often thought-provoking, but seldom drew enough of an audience to keep it going. All his programs were called, simply, "The Dick Cavett Show."

Americans were watching more television than ever before.

There were 77,800,000 TV homes in the United States in 1980; 66,300,000 of them were color TVs; 39,800,000 of them had two or more sets.

There was much, much more to see on television as it entered the '80s.

All this programming, the hours watched, its influence and impact, was escalating with the advent of new technology.

Facing page: Garrett Morris, Bill Murray, and Gilda Radner, original cast members of "Saturday Night Live."

252

Brooke Shields, John Ritter, Bob Hope and "Mr T," working on a sketch for a TV special celebrating Hope's 81st birthday in 1984.

CHAPTER VI

INTO THE FUTURE

Cable television was born of necessity.

Since television signals travel through the air, any obstacles – mountains for instance – may cause some disturbance. In remote areas, where signals may be weak, over-the-air transmission is potentially troublesome. In densely-populated metropolitan areas, tall buildings could be responsible for congested airwaves.

Cable television was introduced, at first, to solve those problems.

It began in June 1948 in Mahanoy City in eastern Pennsylvania, where residents couldn't receive Philadelphia's over-the-air stations because of nearby mountains. John Watson, who worked for Pennsylvania Power & Light and ran an appliance store, strung twin lead wires from a pole to his warehouse at the foot of the mountain and onto his store. He was then able to demonstrate the TV sets he was trying to sell. Along the way he "wired" eight homes for television.

Ed Parsons was aware of a similar reception problem in Astoria, Oregon, on the other side of the nation. He developed a system that allowed him, by November 1948, to pick up signals from a Seattle station three mountain ranges away.

Similar innovation worked in Lansford, Pennsylvania.

Eventually, these small "mom-and-pop" operations were replaced by corporations. Teleprompter, for one, became virtually synonymous with cable in the 1960s.

In parallels similar to the growth of television itself, cable started to see the possibilities of broadcasting its own programs. Also similarly to commercial television, cable turned to sports events to tout its wares.

Time Incorporated set up a cable operation it called Home Box Office (HBO) in 1972. Launched by microwave, HBO's first two programs were a professional hockey game and a movie, "Sometimes a Great Notion" with Paul Newman and Henry Fonda. Three hundred and sixty-five homes in Wilkes-Barre in norhteastern Pennsylvania recieved the transmission. Three years later, heavyweight champion Muhammad Ali fought "Smokey" Joe Frazier in the famous "Thriller in Manila" bout, telecast via satellite by HBO. With that event (Ali retained his title with a knockout), HBO started disseminating sports and uncut movies to a growing national cable system that had become a purveyor of programs rather than just a re-transmitter.

The newsroom of the cable
Satellite News Channel.

256

Satellite televison dishes have added a new dimenson to "the tube."

Cable has offered more choice and better reception to TV viewers.

Satellite transmissions sped up the growth of cable, and satellite networks proliferated in the late 1970s. Ted Turner put his local Atlanta, Georgia station on satellite and created the first "superstation." Television evangelists – "televangelists" in the shortcut of TV jargon – saw the potential, too. Pat Robertson set up a station in 1977 that evolved into the CBN religion network. With the backing of Getty Oil, William and Scott Rasmussen started the all-sports ESPN in 1979.

Cable success has been nothing short of phenomenal.

In 1958, there were four hundred and fifty subscribers reaching 1.1 percent of the television nation. Thirty years later, there were more than forty-seven million in more than half of the country's television households, with revenues approaching $13 billion. Cable's history is now on exhibit at a National Cable Television Center and Museum at The Pennsylvania State University. The memorabilia on display includes a model of the first satellite uplink truck.

At the last count there were sixty cable video networks and more than a dozen more regional cable networks, plus special interest networks providing a multiplicity of program choices.

There's an all-news channel, a channel devoted solely to weather, one for financial news and another for science. Two channels show twenty-four hours of comedy, just comedy! The list goes on. One wit has wondered about the future: all-diet, all-Cher networks?

257

Walter Cronkite, the dean of broadcast journalists.

The Reverend Jerry Falwell on his "Old Time Gospel Hour," a show broadcast on 391 stations.

258

In some places, depending on franchise arrangements with local authorities, there were public access channels set aside for virtually anyone to use. Sometimes that created censorship problems, as purveyors of sexually explicit material took advantage of the opportunity.

In the media capital of New York City in 1990, a cable television subscriber had access to:

- The three major network channels (CBS, NBC, ABC)
- Three local independent channels
- A Public Broadcasting System outlet that included Black Entertainment Television
- A channel devoted to travel news and features
- A Spanish-speaking channel
- The Financial News Network, sharing a channel with the Madison Square Garden sports network
- A local National Education Television network outlet
- A city channel, shared with the City University of New York, for culture, science and humanities
- Lifetime, for women's information and entertainment
- Two public access channels
- A twenty-four hour sports network (ESPN)
- Superstation TBS (Turner Broadcasting System, from Atlanta, Georgia)
- MTV (Music Television), twenty-four hours of music videos
- The choice of several premium-pay movie channels
- USA Network, for family entertainment and sports
- A leased access channel
- Nickleodeon and the Disney channel, for children's programming
- Sports Channel, for local sports
- C-SPAN, a public affairs channel
- A home shopping network channel, shared with Chinese programming
- A twenty-four hour news channel (CNN)
- A&E, for performing arts and entertainment
- VH-1, a twenty-four hour contemporary music station
- Headline news, twenty-four hours in-brief news and information

Cable News Network (CNN), in business since 1980.

Cable Satellite Public Affairs (C-SPAN) at the National Governors Conference in Washington, D.C., in 1985.

260

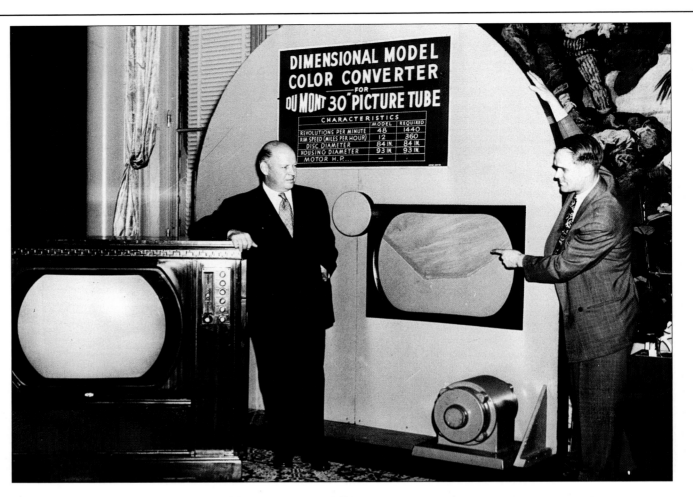

DuMont showing off its color television sets.

Modern TV studio control rooms bear a close resemblance to jetliner cockpits.

– A weather channel

Plus open channels for future possibilities.

Something for everyone.

As of 1990, the ten largest cable networks were:

ESPN (50.1 million subscribers); Cable News Network (49.5 million); WTBS (48.4 million); USA Network (46.1 million); MTV (44.7 million); Nickelodeon (44.4 million); CBN (44.2 million); Nashville Network (43.8 million); C-SPAN (42.6 million); Lifetime (42.5 million).

Turner Entertainment president, Ted Turner, operates four cable networks; TNT (Turner Network Television), TBS (Turner's Atlanta Superstation), the all-news CNN (Cable News Network) and Headline News.

Nam June Palk with his video sculpture Fin de Siécle II *("End of the Century II"), made up of more than three hundred televison sets controlled by a digital computer.*

261

Second-graders receiving a music lesson on their school's closed circuit television system in 1961.

Most successful to date – no surprise – has been the sports network.

Early in 1989, for example, the owner of a cable television set had this choice of sports on one Saturday between noon and midnight: a college basketball game, a sports special showing boxing and speed skating, a golf tournament from Florida, auto racing, more college basketball, bowling, more college basketball or more golf. Then there was always another sports special, with live boxing and taped bobsledding from Italy, professional hockey, World Cup skiing, indoor track and field, or more college basketball. Or perhaps another pro hockey game, a professional basketball game, more pro hockey, or more college basketball.

One day. Just sports. An overdose?

In 1990, the ESPN network alone planned eight professional football games, one hundred and seventy-five baseball games, fifty regular season college football games and five bowl games. In addition, there were two hundred and twenty-five college basketball games and nineteen tournament games, fifteen World Cup ski races, forty golf tournaments and two hundred and thirty auto races. And, as if that little lot weren't enough, thirty-one bowling tournaments, the National Football League draft and Hall of Fame inductions for baseball, basketball and pro football were thrown in for good measure.

That was all in addition to the sports programming provided by the major commercial networks. In 1988, an Olympics year, this alone totaled one thousand, seven hundred and fifty-three hours.

Warner's "Nickleodeon" started in 1979, transmitting five young-people's programs by satellite for thirteen hours each weekday and for fourteen at weekends.

Far left: Jerry Rice diving into the end zone for a San Francisco 49er score during the 1989 Super Bowl, the most watched annual sports show.

265

Left: José Canseco of the Oakland As fitting in a bit of batting practice.

Above: the danger and excitement of the Indianapolis 500, relayed to living rooms by televison.

Left: college post-season bowl games rely heavily on revenue from television.

Left: Kareem Abdul-Jabbar (number 33), one of many sportsmen made into heroes by television.

Arguably the most influential of the contemporary cable output has been – zap! – MTV, an all-music video network born in 1981.

"I want my MTV!" it screamed in its promotion. Apparently its barkers were right, especially among the young. MTV's first few years were successful enough to spawn two affiliated channels, VH-1 and Nickelodeon-Nick at Nite.

Some of MTV's content created controversy, particularly a steamy music video set in a church with Madonna singing "Like a Prayer" and dancing among burning crosses. Then, in the video "If I Could Turn Back Time," Cher was seen aboard the battleship USS *Missouri*, doing her number clad in garter belt and body stocking.

But MTV was destined to become more than just another hit innovation with America's youth; it became the symbol of a television generation. The MTV generation grew up nourished by the tube and able to absorb the bombardment of video images and sounds with pleasure. MTV spoke in a language of imagery, in which dazzle was substance and quick cuts the fashion.

It was high time for *TV Guide* to end its association with early television in its annual tribute to the medium's silliest achievements. A fitting gesture was to replace its nostalgic "J. Fred Muggs" tag in favor of the "Zap Awards," after TV's new remote control devices.

Facing page: Connie Chung, Tom Brokaw and John Chancellor, presenters of NBC's coverage of the Republican National Convention in 1988.

266

Baseball Hall of Famer Pete Rose (on the left), selling autographed plaques, baseballs and bats on a cable TV shopping network with Cable Value Network host Alan Skantz.

Technology made a difference not only in production capabilities, but also in the way programming was delivered. Satellite technology played a major role in this.

Satellite communications go back to the creation by Congress of the Communications Satellite Corporation (COMSAT) in 1963. That in turn helped create Intelsat, a consortium of satellite countries. Then, in 1970, the FCC agreed to allow anyone to apply for permission to build and operate both satellites and their own ground stations.

Cable television operators were already delivering programming to homes directly by satellite. Satellite availability also allowed the creation of superstations, whereby local stations might become national, and even international.

Diversity in methods of transmission (and re-transmission) is minimal, however, compared to the multitude of program choices. Americans today can choose from as many as fifty-three TV stations.

Competition, among commercial networks, local stations and cable systems, has grown equally intense in the rerun market of syndication – the syndication of "The Cosby Show" brought in $500 million. Game shows seem to be syndication favorites. Topping the charts among these are "Jeopardy!" and "Wheel of Fortune," both creations of Merv Griffin and King World Productions, which also owns the Oprah Winfrey talk show. (Griffin had been a game show host and had his own late-night talk show in the early 1960s.)

268

Talk Show host Phil Donahue in lively debate with guests on "Donahue," discussing an allegedly racially-motivated attack.

Vanna White and Pat Sajak, co-hosts of the game show "Wheel of Fortune."

"Jeopardy" contestants guess the questions to go with given answers, a simple idea that has become something of a cottage industry since it began in 1974, with Art Fleming as host. Now with Alex Trebek, who is also executive producer, "Jeopardy" has spawned home board games and even a computer version.

"Wheel of Fortune," a game show based on selecting letters and guessing a word or phrase, even made a celebrity of Vanna White – White wore chic, stylish fashions to turn the letters on the board. Pat Sajak (who replaced Chuck Woolery) was able to parlay his success as "Wheel" host into his own late-night talk show.

"The Oprah Winfrey Show" topped the list of daytime talk shows, which included syndication of "Donahue" and "Sally Jessye Raphael." The latter programs had become popular due to their involvement of the audience in debates on topics as varied

270 *Right: Here he is ... Bert Parks, serenading the audience as master of ceremonies on the "Miss America" pageant, with previous winners Dorothy Benham (on the left) and Mary Ann Mobley.*

Below: "Fat Albert and the Cosby Kids" in 1976.

© FILMATION 1974

as marriage, infidelity, gays, drugs, weight control and politics.

Fashionable on the syndication market for a while were reality-based shows, often referred to as "tabloid television" for their emphasis on celebrity scandals and shock-value stories. These included magazine-style shows like "A Current Affair," "Hard Copy" and "Inside Edition," kind of kicking cousins to "trash" television, or "insult TV." Insult TV had been made infamous by Morton Downey Jr. and Geraldo Rivera, to whom confrontation was the goal and antagonism the means. One "Geraldo" show resulted in a broken nose for the host after a fight broke out with guests. In another, ex-wives of stars, including those of Dustin Hoffman, Vidal Sassoon and Robert Goulet, talked about breaking up with their rich and famous husbands.

The Fox Broadcasting Company tried to develop itself into a true "fourth network" in competition with ABC, CBS and NBC. It started up in 1987 and won a relatively loyal following with its bold and sometimes brassy productions. Among these were the

271

Shooting a scene for "Secret Passions," billed as a gay soap opera.

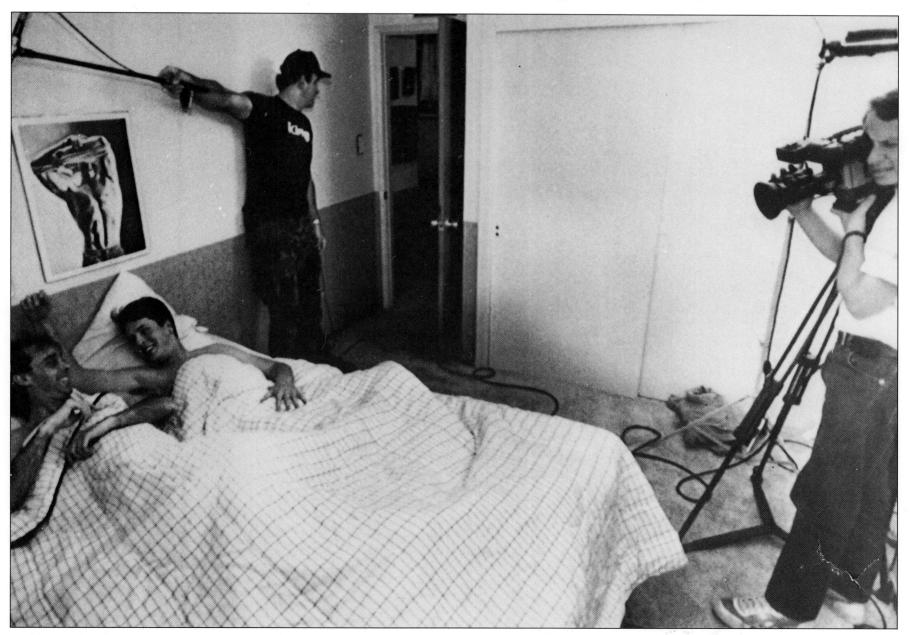

272

Madonna in her "Like a Prayer" video.

The cast of Fox Televison's often controversial "Married with Children."

teen-oriented police show, "21 Jump Street" and "Married ... With Children," a situation "comedy" described by one critic as having "all the warmth of a boa constrictor." Fox also produced "The Tracey Ullman Show," a variety series imported from Britain, and several gritty "reality" programs.

More competition – and more choice – came with the creation of home videos and videotape recorders. The first practical VCRs (videocassette recorders) were introduced in the early 1950s, but it wasn't until the mid-1970s that the home video revolution really kicked off. It was brought about by Sony's consumer-acceptable home taping system. VCRs enabled the viewer to tape programs of their choice and play them back at a time more convenient for watching.

It all seemed to come full circle when homemade videos provided the program material for ABC's "America's Funniest Home Videos," which began in 1989 and achieved "instant" popularity.

Prerecorded movies appeared in 1980 with a deal between Magnetic Video and 20th Century Fox for fifty movies, including "Patton," "The French Connection" and "The Sound of Music." A few years later, video stores and rental videos began to appear and home television sets took on another new function; many sets were already serving as monitors for computer games.

Commercial television felt the competition deeply. Where once the three major networks had had a virtual monopoly on the national viewing audience, their prime-time numbers now dropped sharply, from eighty percent in 1985 to sixty-eight percent in 1989. That figure still indicated tremendous viewing numbers, however. When it came to "The Cosby Show," those numbers were exceptional. It was hailed as the most successful prime-time show of the '80s.

A former stand-up comic, Bill Cosby was no stranger to television. Between 1965 and 1968 he had co-starred with Robert Culp on "I Spy" – the first starring role for a black on a regular American Drama TV series. He had also guest-starred on the children's show "The Electric Company" in the '70s. Furthermore, he was executive producer on, and host of, a Saturday-morning cartoon series called "Fat Albert and the Cosby Kids" (later known as "The New Fat Albert Show"). In it he introduced characters from his Philadelphia childhood, such as "Fat Albert" himself, "Mushmouth," and "Weird Harold," and always finished with a moral about growing up. He had also earned a reputation as an author, mostly on child-rearing, *and* starred in the situation comedy "The Bill Cosby Show," as a high school gym teacher.

274

By the time his proposal for "The Cosby Show" was accepted by NBC, he was in a position to insist on total creative control. He used it to mold his own educational and child-rearing theories into

Bill Cosby (on the right) and Robert Culp as American secret agents in "I Spy," which ran from 1965 to 1968.

a gentle family comedy. No stereotypical black family here. Cosby plays a gynecologist, his wife (played by Phylicia Rashad) an attorney. The pair raise five children, with love, attention ... and intelligent, witty, funny scripts.

"The Cosby Show" first appeared in 1984 and quickly became the season's prime-time phenomenon. It has remained at or near the top of the ratings chart ever since.

Cosby parlayed the show's success into syndication, new books, the spinoff show "A Different World" and commercials (Jell-O and Kodak being the better known). In doing so he earnt the credit of "most successful entertainer in history" from *TV Guide*.

A *Forbes* business magazine list estimated Cosby's total earnings during the 1988-1989 period at $95 million – second only to those of pop star Michael Jackson and movie-maker Stephen Spielberg in the entertainment industry category. The highest-paid woman entertainer on that list was Oprah Winfrey, with estimated total earnings of $55 million, beating Johnny Carson

"The Cosby Show" family.

276

Talk Show hostess Oprah Winfrey showing off her new slimmer figure on national television in 1988. She had lost sixty-seven pounds to fit into a pair of size ten jeans.

who came in with just $45 million for the same period.

Carson was still going strong, though not as regularly, as the host of the "Tonight" show, which he had taken over in 1962. Carson also serves as an author, a performer in night clubs and as president of Carson Productions.

Oprah Winfrey has found success as hostess of her own daytime talk show, to the point where she has become an international celebrity and perhaps the richest woman on television. Winfrey has been reported to be worth $250 million, including her earnings as an actress and TV producer. It has also been reported that the company that syndicates her show has a $50 million to $70 million insurance policy on her life. She has made headlines herself, mostly about her weight problem. After gaining fame for losing sixty-seven pounds, she then garnered notoriety acknowledging that she had in fact put seventeen pounds back on. *TV Guide* once superimposed her face on the more svelte body of actress Ann-Margret.

Oprah is a prime and positive example to women on – and in – television. Studies show that television programs, highlighted by prime-time situation comedies, feature more and more women than ever before: working women; working mothers; older women and stronger black women.

What was happening in society in general was not the only reason for the changes, perhaps not even the key reason. Sponsors and program executives alike were aware of a shift toward a majority of female viewers in prime-time ratings, just as men appeared to move to cable offerings. What's more, women were the main buyers of the products most advertised by prime-time sponsors – cosmetics and household goods.

Whatever the reasons, in the '80s women appeared in more positive roles on the screen and in more influential roles behind the camera too; more women produced shows, more women wrote scripts.

Ahead in the results were "Roseanne," "Murphy Brown," "Designing Women" and "The Golden Girls."

In "Roseanne," created and produced by Roseanne Barr, the comedy revolves around a blue-collar working woman, who is also the wise-cracking matriarch of a family with three children. "Roseanne" makes much of the burdens of a working mom. John Goodman plays her husband.

Dolly Parton (top center) in a guest appearance on "Designing Women" in 1989. Delta Burke and Meshach Taylor flank Ms Parton, Joan Smart, Dixie Carter and Annie Potts (from left to right) are on the couch.

277

Roseanne has set a record for magazine cover appearances, her show hit No. 1 in the ratings race and her autobiography, "Roseanne: My Life as a Woman," has also made the best-seller list. The turmoils of her personal life, from marriage to weight control, could provide fodder for years of soap opera scripts.

Candice Bergen plays the witty but real anchorwoman of the fictional "FYI" news team, the fulcrum of the hip and topical "Murphy Brown," created and produced by Diane English.

"Designing Women" follows the lives of four Southern women who run their own decorating business. The series' sharp scripts, virtually all written by Linda Bloodworth-Thomason since the show began in 1986, take on strong, contemporary themes each week, though not without humor.

"The Golden Girls," a popular comedy starring Bea Arthur (formerly TV's "Maude"), is about four women of a certain age living in Florida.

A 1988 episode of "Roseanne," starring (from left to right) George Clooney as Booker, John Goodman as Dan, Roseanne Barr in the title role, and Laurie Metcalf as Jackie.

278

A female star is the centerpiece of "Murder, She Wrote," in which Angela Lansbury plays a Down East mystery writer who gets involved in solving crimes herself.

It's all a long, long way from "Charlie's Angels," a late 1970s show about female detectives. This was described by many as the "jiggle show," for its exploitation of the pulchritude of stars Farrah Fawcett, Kate Jackson, Jaclyn Smith and Cheryl Ladd.

"The Golden Girls," (from left) Betty White as Rose, Bea Arthur as Dorothy and Rue McClanahan as Blanche.

280 *Stars of "Roseanne," John Goodman and Roseanne Barr.*

Bruce Willis and Cybil Shepherd, co-starring in "Moonlighting."

The '80s had other popular series: "Moonlighting" was an imaginative 1985 series from ABC which paired Cybill Shepherd and Bruce Willis as an unlikely pair of detectives. She played a beautiful, former fashion model turned owner of a private eye agency, he a wisecracking employee. Stylish repartee and unconventional production helped make it a huge hit in its first two years.

"Cheers," another ensemble situation comedy, also has the advantage of witty scripts, added to sexual innuendo from baseball player turned macho bartender Sam Malone (Ted Danson).

Willis and Shepherd, unlikely partners in "Moonlighting."

Targets for Sam's charm include the naive, erudite waitress (Shelley Long) and, more recently, the new manageress of the bar (Kristie Alley). "Cheers" began in 1982 and has gained a loyal following for its camaraderie at the Boston bar of the title, where "everybody knows your name," as the program theme goes.

Daytime soaps continue to lure followers, with the venerable "As the World Turns," "All My Children," "Santa Barbara" and "General Hospital" filling more than their quota of melodrama. The marriage of Luke and Laura (Anthony Geary and Genie Francis) on "General Hospital" in 1981 was as highly publicized as a royal coronation.

Night-time soaps seem to have evolved into a new format, exemplified by "L.A. Law" with its ongoing stories and characters

282

The regulars on "Cheers."

Original cast members of the daytime soap "As the World Turns," which began in 1956.

without the usual melodrama. "Wiseguy," "China Beach" and even "thirtysomething" fit the category that may have started with "Rich Man, Poor Man: Book II."

"Family Ties" called it quits after seven seasons as one of TV's most popular family comedy series.

"Miami Vice," the pop police series that made a sex symbol of Don Johnson, made its debut in September 1984. Five years later, the series had fired its last bullets and become so popular that an auction was held for the props, including pastel (of course) place mats and art deco furniture. It was a hip, stylish series set on Florida's Gold Coast. Don Johnson and Philip Michael Thomas played Crockett and Tubbs, dashing vice-squad detectives. They dressed in expensive, colorful clothing, drove around in

284

Philip Michael Thomas and Don Johnson, stars of "Miami Vice."

Ken Olin, Mel Harris and baby, cast members of the unusual but critically acclaimed "thirtysomething."

expensive cars and solved their cases in glamorous settings to the sound of pulsating rock music.

(When the series "Golden Girls" began, in-jokesters called it "Miami Nice.")

"Hill Street Blues" was a tough, provocative police series that pulled no punches either in language or realism. It centered on the station house in an urban ghetto area and weaved several stories together each week. The regular cast included Daniel J. Travanti as Captain Frank Furillo and Veronica Hamel as a public defender (there was also some romantic interest between the two). Michael Conrad played the head sergeant who ended each morning's roll call with: "And hey, let's be careful out there."

The television miniseries, popular in earlier years with the likes of "Roots," "Shogun," "Winds of War" and "The Thorn Birds," made something of a comeback in 1989 with the Western, "Lonesome Dove." Based on Larry McMurtry's Pulitzer Prize winning book, the eight-hour saga was shown over four nights and achieved the biggest audience for a miniseries in five years – watched in an estimated 25.7 million homes.

Facing page: co-stars of the gritty police series "Hill Street Blues": Michael Conrad, Veronica Hamel and Daniel J. Travanti (standing).

286

Stars of "L.A. Law," Corbin Benson (seated), Jill Eikenberry and Harry Hamlin.

Below: a struggle aboard ship between Geraldine Brooks, David Janssen (center) and John Larkin during an episode of "The Fugitive."

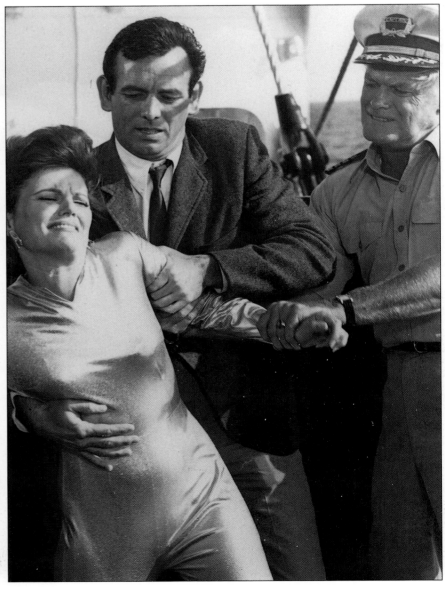

There has also been a new entry among the nighttime talk shows, "Late Night with David Letterman." This is often more of a parody than a competitor in its field. Letterman presents, to phrase it mildly, a non-conventional interview style on a show with a rambling format. However the show is described, the sneaker-wearing host himself has gained a loyal, almost "cult," following.

British television has provided some of the most critically praised material for American audiences.

Public broadcasting's long-running, British-made "Mystery" series was introduced in 1981, its plots often taken from Agatha Christie and featuring first Vincent Price as host and later Diana Rigg.

Hog Chief, a prize-winning boar, making a guest appearance on "Late Night with David Letterman" in 1987.

288

"Fawlty Towers," perhaps best described as "high vaudeville," starred John Cleese, one of the Monty Python troupe, as the owner of a resort hotel.

"Tinker, Tailor, Soldier, Spy" and "Smiley's People" starred Alec Guinness as the master spy of John Le Carré's books.

Even "Yes, Prime Minister," a decidedly British satire on politics, won approval on American public television outlets. In Britain, a cat at the Cabinet Office in London was named "Humphrey," after Sir Humphrey Appleby in the series. Politicians seem to be universally understood no matter what the form of government.

Television news and documentaries, public affairs shows and discussion programs, remain at the heart of the medium's purpose - to inform and elucidate. Surveys have shown that most of what we know is gained from television. At the beginning of the '90s, forty million people watched the evening news over some fourteen hundred stations.

Vanna White, of "Wheel of Fortune" fame, spins her introduction of NBC Entertainment President Brandon Tartikoff during the network's press week gathering in 1988.

290

CBS news correspondent
Edward R. Murrow, reporting
on the 1956 national election.

Rhoda and Joe, played by
Valerie Harper and David
Groh, were married on a 1975
episode of "Rhoda."

Stars of the "Lou Grant" series: (from left) Edward Asner in the title role as newspaper city editor, Nancy Marchand as publisher Margaret Pynchon, and Mason Adams as managing editor Charlie Hume.

Redd Foxx (on the left) starred as Fred Sanford, with Desmond Wilson as his son Lamont, in "Sanford and Son," which ran for five years from 1972.

The children of this era can truthfully say they were present at the revolution, because of television. Television has recorded history being made, from natural disasters to political revolutions. As prescient as TV's early pioneers were, they probably could not have imagined their "radio-with-pictures" bringing such momentous events, live and direct, into our homes. Viewers in recent times have been able to watch the walls come tumbling down all over Eastern Europe. In Romania, where the government television station had once beamed the glory of leader Nicolae Ceausescu to a numbed nation, TV became the voice and the soul of the revolution, broadcasting Ceausescu's capture and execution. Viewers were able to see a lone young man stand up to a row of Chinese tanks in Tiananmen Square, and Nelson Mandela walk from a prison in South Africa a free man. Even South African Broadcasting telecast his release live, unprecedented for a spot news development in that country.

Many learned about these international events on the news

292 *Television crews covered the student occupation of Tiananmen Square in Beijing in May 1989, but the Chinese authorities banned satellite broadcasts.*

show "Nightline," with host Ted Koppel. Begun in 1980, the show reaches more than five million viewers nightly, and is considered by many to be the most influential news program on television. ABC's "World News Tonight" with Peter Jennings, "NBC Nightly News" with Tom Brokaw, and Dan Rather's "CBS Evening News" also broadcast details, as did a myriad of morning news shows.

Where can television go from here? The crystal ball is clear on some things:

Its future will be shaped by technology. New hardware and software will determine how programs will be delivered to the home.

Ugly images of the Vietnam War were brought onto our television screens on a daily basis.

Television screens will be bigger – and still bigger. And smaller, too: hand-held sets, like Sony's pocket-size equivalent of the Walkman, are already available.

Images will be sharper. HDTV – high definition television – has already been introduced. It can provide image definition of more than a thousand lines. That would mean the bigger screens could offer better quality pictures than smaller ones do now. A step beyond HDTV is fiber optics, whereby video programming is transmitted through a glass strand where copper cable couldn't handle the band width.

Sound quality will improve as well; nineteen percent of American households already have TV sets with stereo sound. Q-Sound is a new three-dimensional stereo innovation that makes sound seem to be coming from different angles.

Cable systems will continue to grow, providing greater choices in both entertainment and enlightenment.

The use of satellite service in combination with cable and local

294

ABC's Ted Koppel (on the left) and Peter Jennings, in 1985.

broadcast will result in more superstations able to send local signals throughout the country, and perhaps the globe. Individual satellite dishes, some as small as a foot in diameter, already point skyward from farmland and city rooftop to grope for satellite transmissions.

Home video is set to add to viewing possibilities, either by cassette or laser videodisc.

TV will serve as a data retrieval system, combining with computer technology to provide access to information from spot news to history.

A computerized dial-in service, through which one may telephone to see a program of one's choice – from a Broadway play to a Super Bowl, has already been initiated.

Pay-per-view is already here. In pay-per-view television, viewers pay a fee to get a one-time program, like a movie. It has been promoted as the television technology of the future, especially for sports, because of its potential for profit making. It has been

295

Peter Jennings, anchoring "World News Tonight" from Moscow, in February 1986.

296

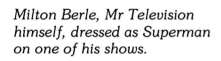

Milton Berle, Mr Television himself, dressed as Superman on one of his shows.

estimated that, if the Super Bowl were provided only in this way, $500 million or more would be generated in revenue.

NBC and its cable television partner, Cablevision Systems Corporation, offered the Summer Olympics (six hundred commercial-free hours) for $100 to $150 per view, hoping to take as much as $325 million from subscribers to the event. (It cost NBC $401 million for the TV rights to the Olympics.)

Nearly eighteen million American homes already receive pay-per-view programming, and it is estimated that this figure will reach 23.6 million in just a couple of years.

If TV does indeed link the world, the links will surely get closer as the increasing growth of television in other countries sees more exchanges and thus develops a better understanding between those countries. In 1990, more than a hundred public broadcast stations in the United States presented "Vremya" (the Russian word for time), the Soviet evening news program watched by an estimated one hundred and fifty million people in that country. It

Filming the "Today" show in 1990, with co-hosts Bryant Gumbel and Deborah Norville.

President Ronald Reagan at the podium of the Dallas Convention Center, in person and reproduced on a huge screen, during his acceptance speech at the 1984 Republican National Convention.

lacked the slick production to which the U.S. audiences have become accustomed, but the straightforward presentation nevertheless gave them an unprecedented insight into Soviet society.

The "explosion" of programming choices will continue to fragment audiences, to the point of personally tailored television, already a reality. The concept is to computer-profile a subscriber's television tastes, tape-record those programs of interest, and play them back upon request.

Technology will indeed change the form of television's future. But the substance? That is not as clear. Television is all things to all people. But what do we want from it?

As Edward R. Murrow once said of television: "The instrument can teach, it can illuminate; yes, it can even inspire. But it can do those things only to the extent that humans are determined to use it to those ends. Otherwise, it is merely lights and wires in a box."

Will we learn to use the medium wisely, or will we allow it to use us?

Will it increase our knowledge and understanding of each other and the world we live in? Or become our push-button opiate?

Will Sam Malone ever get married on "Cheers"? Will someone else try to shoot J.R.?

Tune in next week.

But first ... these words:

THE END

300

"The Late Show with Joan Rivers," with the hostess (on the right) having a sing song with Cher and Pee Wee Herman, accompanied on the piano by Elton John.